QUESTION AND ANSWER GUIDE

£7.95 D

Gov... t and Politics

Q&A

Neil McNaughton

Philip Allan Updates
Market Place
Deddington
Oxfordshire
OX15 0SE

tel: 01869 338652
fax: 01869 337590
e-mail: sales@philipallan.co.uk
www.philipallan.co.uk

ISBN 0 86003 774 6

Cover illustration by John Spencer

Printed by Raithby, Lawrence & Co Ltd, Leicester

Contents

Introduction

The topics

Introduction

This question and answer guide has been written as a companion for AS government and politics students. It is suitable for the three major examination boards in England and Wales. Although the style of questions used by the boards varies, there are sufficient common features to use examples from all three. The book is intended to help you to organise notes, plan revision and, above all, to practise the kind of questions you are likely to face in the examinations. It is a general guide on how to approach different kinds of question, with specific points on what to do and what not to do.

There are exam-style questions on each topic covered by the specifications. Every question is followed by a mark scheme, plus one or two example student answers interspersed with examiner's comments (preceded by the icon e). There are two main ways in which these questions can be used:

(1) Answer the question using your notes and, possibly, material from textbooks and other sources. Be careful to limit the length of your answers to the amount you would be able to write in the time allowed under examination conditions. This method is probably more appropriate for those topics you find difficult.

(2) Plan how you intend to answer the question, decide what to include, attempt to commit the content to memory and then answer the question under examination conditions.

Having undertaken these exercises, it is important to review your own performance against the criteria shown. You should note the serious omissions and errors, comparing your answers with the best examples shown. Do not look at the best example answers and then seek to reproduce them, because it is unlikely that identical questions will appear in the exam and you must be flexible in your approach. This guide is designed to help with content and technique; it is *not* a set of model answers.

General guidance on answering questions

Before using the example questions and answers, make sure that you understand the general guidance on answering different kinds of question.

Obeying command words

Every question contains a specific command and it is crucial that you obey these commands. If you do not, you could lose up to 40% of the marks available. Of course, there may be commands other than those mentioned below but, whatever they may be, it is vital that candidates respond to them in their answers. Such responses need not always be extensive. The key point is that a response is attempted.

Describe/explain, what is meant by...?

In this case you should do the following:

- define clearly
- explain different uses
- give some real examples
- give any well-known opinions

Example: 'Describe (or explain) the doctrine of individual ministerial responsibility.'

Define The doctrine of individual ministerial responsibility is a principle which suggests that a minister is accountable to parliament for the policies and major decisions made within his or her department. It implies that ministers must justify policies and decisions, explain them and take responsibility for errors. In extreme cases, a minister may be expected to resign.

Usages Originally the doctrine was specific in that ministers resigned as a matter of honour, and to protect the anonymity of their civil servants. It has come to mean that ministers must account for what happens in the department, but only have to resign when they are directly responsible. They are not responsible for operational matters beyond their direct control.

Examples The best-known example of the original operation of the doctrine was Lord Carrington's resignation as foreign secretary after Argentina invaded the Falkland Islands in 1982 because British forces were not ready to repel the invasion. Michael Howard's refusal to resign as home secretary in the 1990s over a series of prison security failures demonstrated that the doctrine is falling into disuse.

Opinions Most commentators suggest that the doctrine no longer works unless a minister is politically weak, loses the support of the prime minister, or completely loses the support of parliament. Ministers like Michael Howard and Lord Falconer (the Dome minister) appear to believe that the doctrine of individual ministerial responsibility has little relevance.

Distinguish between...

Do not simply describe the points in turn and hope the examiner can pick out what distinguishes them. Instead:

- pick out the distinguishing features and describe them
- try to distinguish between the important and minor differences
- point out any distinctions which may be blurred
- use examples where necessary

Example: 'Distinguish between the role of a party and a pressure group.'

Distinguishing features Parties seek governmental power; pressure groups do not. Parties put candidates up for election whereas pressure groups rarely do. Parties have to develop a range of policies for all government responsibilities, whereas pressure groups normally have narrower aims and policies. It is necessary for parties to take responsibility for their policies if they form a government. Pressure groups are not burdened by such responsibility.

Importance of distinctions The distinctions shown above are all important and help to draw a clear dividing line. There are other, less important examples. Parties tend to have more formal organisations than pressure groups, and are usually better financed. Democratic parties also have to act legally, while some extreme pressure groups such as the Animal Rights movement sometimes operate outside the law.

Blurred distinctions Some pressure groups have put up candidates at local and general elections and so appear to behave like parties. This is true of the Green movement, which is now a recognised party. Single-issue parties such as the UK Independence Party and the Referendum Party are more like pressure groups in reality. Large pressure groups, such as the Confederation of British Industry (CBI) or trade unions, behave very much like parties in certain respects (and some have more members too) and develop a wide range of policy, often outside their own immediate interests.

Is/are... ?

This apparently straightforward question is not so simple. You will need to:

- include any authoritative opinions you know
- put both sides of the argument, but...
- ...come to a definite conclusion — yes or no

Example: 'Is the prime minister now effectively a president?'

Authoritative opinions Some commentators now describe the British prime minister as virtually a president. Tony Benn, for example, has argued this point for over 20 years and Michael Foley calls the prime minister's position the 'British presidency'. Several former ministers under Margaret Thatcher — including Geoffrey Howe and Nigel Lawson — also made this complaint. There are others (George Jones and Peter Hennessy, for example) who disagree, suggesting that, while there is a more presidential style, there is not the presidential substance to match.

Both sides State the arguments that the prime minister is more powerful than ever before, owing to the effects of media coverage and the growing importance of external relations including Europe. There is an increasing leadership orientation within all the parties. The growth of the Cabinet Office as a kind of prime minister's department (not unlike the White House) is supplemented with agencies and private advisers who serve the prime minister. On the other side of the argument are the limitations imposed by the ruling party, parliament and the cabinet, which are largely absent in the case of a true presidency. Note that the prime minister owes his or her authority to parliament and that this can be withdrawn. A president has authority from the people directly.

Conclusion State either that the growth of prime ministerial power does make the prime minister much like a president, despite the limitations described, or that the many limitations mean that, although the prime minister's power has grown, he or she can never be truly compared to a president.

To what extent...? How effectively...? How much...?

- explain why the question might be asked
- describe the main political processes involved
- give some estimate of the extent or the effectiveness of 'how much' and explain why you have come to that conclusion
- give as many examples or illustrations as you can
- the answers may range from 'totally' to 'hardly at all'; it doesn't matter which so long as you can justify the answer

Example: 'How effective is the judiciary in protecting rights in the UK?

Why is the question asked? Explain that rights protection has become a key issue and that this throws into focus the role of the courts. The Human Rights Act has placed even more emphasis on the role of the judiciary. For these reasons the effectiveness of judges and the courts has been called into question.

Main political processes Describe the role of the courts including the processes of judicial review, the upholding of common law rights and the operation of the Human Rights Act and the European Convention.

Estimates of 'extent' Note that there are many judicial reviews but few succeed. Note that courts cannot challenge legislation and so common law is weak. However, speculate that courts have much more power with the Human Rights Act and can strike down Scottish and Welsh executive decisions, Scottish legislation, local authority decisions and actions by departments and other public bodies. Note the lack of jurisdiction over prerogative powers.

Examples Possibly highlight the 17 cases lost by home secretary, Michael Howard, over prisoners' rights in the 1990s. Note also how the press has asserted its rights to publish information (the Shayler case, the Crossman diaries). Quote examples such as the Government Communications Headquarters (GCHQ) case to illustrate the courts' weakness in asserting rights, and note the extensions of police powers through legislation to illustrate how courts cannot challenge parliamentary sovereignty.

Conclusion With the evidence to support the case, this could be anything from an assertion that courts are weak to the idea that they have great strength. Perhaps suggest that the Human Rights Act will enhance their power.

Why ...?

- state why the question is being asked
- explain the factors which lead to the conclusion
- ensure that you have arrived at a 'because' answer
- justify 'because' with as much illustration as possible

Example: 'Why are some pressure groups more successful than others?'
Why is the question asked? Discuss the importance of pressure groups in a democracy, showing how the successful ones can determine the ways in which governments react to conflicts and which policies are likely to be adopted. They also explain why some groups in society can gain advantages over others.

The factors leading to a conclusion These will include descriptions of pressure groups that mobilise public opinion (e.g. fuel lobby, green lobby), have large resources (e.g. big business lobbies), are well organised (e.g. the Countryside Alliance), use public figures successfully (e.g. gay rights, AIDS) or have media support. Describe the insider/outsider argument with examples such as the CBI and the National Farmers' Union (NFU) as insiders, and Greenpeace and Animal Rights groups as outsiders. Also note which groups are successful with different parties, e.g. unions with Labour, rural/agricultural groups with the Conservatives.

Because A critical account of which factors are most important, possibly challenging conventional views such as insider/outsider status or suggesting that the factors shown above are the main reasons for success or failure. It may also be that groups simply capture the public mood (e.g. the anti-poll tax lobby).

Justify Pick out the successful pressure groups in the current period, such as Greenpeace over genetically modified (GM) food, the Countryside Alliance over fox-hunting, the betting industry over betting tax removal, and welfare groups over attacks on poverty. Demonstrate their success.

Essay writing

The traditional 40 or 45-minute essay is not part of AS assessment. Nevertheless, some of the questions, usually (c) or (d) sections of stepped questions, have a considerable number of marks and therefore time allocated to them. They require what are effectively mini-essays. The same principles apply for these as for the longer pieces of writing which will be needed for those going on to A2 politics.

Planning an essay

Planning essays is a wise technique, whether for set assignments without a time constraint or under examination conditions. Planning may be time-consuming, but it is likely to save time in the long run and pays dividends in terms of marks.

A plan can be as little as a few bullet points or as much as a full-scale plan or mind map. Any plan can help with the learning process, but in the exam room it is a way of determining your essay structure that can help you to avoid leaving out key points. As an additional incentive, plans may also gain a few extra marks. Examiners look at a plan and if anything contained in it is not subsequently included in the essay, this can be given credit. Furthermore, in the unhappy event that you run out of time and cannot attempt a full-scale answer, a good plan is a way of salvaging a few of the marks lost due to time mismanagement.

A word of caution is needed here. The chances that an essay set in the examination is identical to one you have previously planned are quite small. Resist the temptation to write the essay you have planned rather than the one that is set. It is important to adapt your material to the exact demands of the question.

Structuring a mini-essay

It is often said that essays should have a beginning, a middle and an end. This may seem obvious, but it is certainly true. Although there are no marks specifically allocated for the structure of an essay, there are marks for powers of expression and how well you can explain an argument or frame a discussion. Structure is therefore important.

The beginning

It is good practice to explain how you intend to answer the question. The examiner then gains the impression that you understand what you are being asked and it also helps you to settle down.

Here are two introductions to answers to the question: **'Assess the extent to which pressure groups are positive elements in a modern democracy.'**

In modern pluralist political systems it seems clear that pressure groups must play a vital role in the democratic process. They can, among other functions, provide opportunities for public participation, act as two-way channels of communication between government and the people, and play an important educational role. Nevertheless, some have pointed out problems, especially when small but wealthy and well-organised groups gain a disproportionate amount of influence. To decide, therefore, whether their role is positive, we need to examine their activities and compare the positive and negative elements before reaching a conclusion.

This paragraph serves two functions. It is a brief answer, summarising the points to come, and it is also a plan. Each of the elements in the introduction can now be expanded upon with appropriate examples.

The introduction below does not reach a specific conclusion. However, it is perfectly acceptable to answer the question directly in a first paragraph, as follows:

There is no doubt that modern pressure groups play a major positive role in a democratic system. There are, of course, some negative aspects to their activities but, on balance, the positives outweigh the negatives. We should now examine these factors in more detail.

This serves less well as a plan, but is nonetheless a decisive and clear opening.

The middle

The major part of the essay is the full development of an answer to the question. The specific response to the question, 'Why?' or 'To what extent?' or 'Evaluate' will largely be made at the beginning and the end. The middle explains the evidence, describes the various views there might be on the subject and gives examples and illustrations to back up the evidence.

The middle of the essay about pressure groups should explain the positive aspects of their activities with plenty of illustrations from the real political world. It should also explain counter views and attempt to balance them out. It should express how the situation has changed in the modern period and differentiate between the important and less important aspects of the question. To summarise, the middle of the essay is likely to contain all or most of the following:

- explanations of both sides to an argument
- examples and illustrations to underpin the arguments
- any well-known views on the issue
- some evaluation of what the important aspects of the question are and why
- descriptions of how realities and arguments have changed
- any other relevant facts or issues

The end

This should confirm the answer to the question, even if all elements of the answer were given in the introduction. More importantly still, it should be a firm conclusion. If the question was 'Why?', the answer should be 'because', with the reasons stated clearly. If the question was 'To what extent?', the answer should be something like, 'a great deal' or 'very little' or some other evaluation. Weak conclusions do not necessarily spoil an essay, but they can tip the balance when the examiner is awarding marks for analysis and evaluation.

It should also be stressed that no marks are awarded specifically for personal opinion. It is acceptable to give an opinion as to what conclusions can be reached from the factual evidence you have described, but the conclusion must always be based on firm evidence and not on your own views. A good conclusion would be:

Despite the reservations outlined above, the balance of evidence indicates that pressure groups play a positive role in a democratic society.

This is much better than a bland statement at the end (or indeed at the beginning) which says simply:

I personally think that pressure groups play a positive role in a democratic society.

Unconventional approaches

There is no set formula for writing an exam essay. What is shown above is a safe model, though it is perfectly possible to achieve a high mark by using a less conventional approach. However, the cardinal rules remain:

- make sure you address and respond to the question
- make sure your points are supported by hard evidence
- use real-world examples to illustrate your answer
- express ideas about change whenever this is appropriate

Marks will be sacrificed if these rules are not followed.

Other examination tips

There are some small but nevertheless important tips to follow in the examination room.

Do

- Address the questions directly.
- Make a plan before starting a longer answer. Even if it is only a few bullet points it will help clear your thoughts.
- Make sure you read *all* stimulus material carefully and try to respond to all aspects of it.
- Come to a clear conclusion where the question demands one. Give a balanced and specific answer to the question.
- Finish off an answer with bullet points if you are running out of time.
- Write with a good pen, using black or dark blue ink.
- Balance your time according to the mark allocations.

Do not

- Cross out your plan. Anything of relevance in it might gain some credit.
- Begin writing straight away. Instead stay calm, read the whole examination paper and plan which questions you will attempt and how much time you have for each.
- Spend excessive amounts of time on some questions and run out of time for others.
- Leave out any questions or sections of questions. You must be able to say something about each question, if only for the few marks which may make all the difference to your grade.

Answering stimulus–response questions

Students tend to find stimulus–response questions the most challenging, more because they are not sure how to go about answering them than due to a lack of knowledge. There are a number of procedures which can help.

- Make sure you read *all* the material. It is tempting to rush and start to answer questions before absorbing the information properly. Time spent looking carefully at the stimulus will be well spent. Where statistical data are involved, make sure you understand what the figures are showing. Look especially closely at the headings of columns of figures.
- Consider *all* the material carefully because everything is likely to be relevant to the questions. Apparently minor pieces of statistical information may well be significant. For example, if election statistics are used, do not ignore voting figures for the smaller parties. Any comments you can make about them may well attract additional marks.
- When questions state *specifically* that you are to use *only* the stimulus material, you should follow the instruction. Short direct quotations are fine, but you should express answers using your own words.

- Stick to the time limitations. The marks indicate the relative importance of each section and should act as a strict guide. Marks cannot be transferred from one section to another, so a particularly strong answer cannot compensate for a weaker one.
- When questions do not refer to the stimulus material at all, answers should contain information from both your own knowledge and from the stimulus material.

Revision guide

As a general rule, spend more time on the topics in which you are weak than on those in which you are strong. It is obviously tempting to spend time on your better subjects, but these are the ones which need less time.

In a descriptive subject such as politics it is useful to divide revision into three phases:

Phase 1
With about 3 months to go, read through your notes, textbooks and other materials. Look at the example answers in this book. Do not attempt to learn anything.

Phase 2
About 6 weeks before the exam, sort your notes into good order and fill in any gaps. Try to reduce each topic to a series of headings with condensed descriptions and examples to illustrate each section.

Phase 3
About 2 weeks before the exam, learn the headings and key pieces of information. By now, each heading and key word should call to mind the rest of the material.

An example of a condensed revision sheet for **referenda** might look like this:

Arguments for

Direct democracy — single currency issue
Popular consent — Northern Ireland agreement
Government difficulties — European Community membership 1975
Entrench constitutional change — devolution
e-democracy — possible future issues, cheap and quick

Arguments against

Complex issues — single currency
Emotional response — single currency, death penalty
Media influence — Europe
Financial influence - Scottish vote on Clause 28
Political institutions in disrepute — electoral system
Expense — any
Close results — Welsh devolution
Low turnout — Welsh devolution

Use in the UK

Europe — 1975, possibly on currency
Devolution — Wales, Scotland, Northern Ireland
London mayor
Northern Ireland — Good Friday Agreement
Local votes — on council taxes and expenditure, on elected mayors

The revision scheme above contains most of the points which are likely to be needed. The material is flexible enough to be capable of adaptation for specific questions and there are actual or potential examples to be used.

Active revision

Some lucky students can simply read through written material and have it organised in their memory. For most of us this does not work. The solution is to make revision active. Some ways of doing this are:

- Read through your work and then use it to write out the kind of practice questions shown in this book.
- Write out flash cards or lists on sheets. If necessary, do this more than once.
- Keep condensing material into smaller and smaller forms, from a paragraph to a sentence to a single word.
- Many visual learners use colour and pictorial images. Mind-mapping is also useful for visual learners. It is possible to reduce most key topics to such diagrams.
- Use friends or family to test you on your learning. When revising with a fellow student, it is probably better to use someone at your own approximate level of knowledge and ability. Choosing a stronger student may dishearten you.
- Revising in groups of more than two is rarely a good idea. It may be more sociable, but you will get less work done.
- Revise in small chunks of time. It is generally better to have frequent breaks than to try to revise for a long time and then quit altogether for the rest of the day. Attention spans usually vary from 30 minutes to 2 hours. When you know what your best attention span is, stick to it.

Questions and Answers

This section is divided into ten topic areas that are common to all examination boards (with the exception of voting behaviour, which is not part of the Edexcel specification). Each topic has the following features:

(1) Sample examination questions which are either stimulus–response questions or stepped questions.

(2) Mark allocations for each part of a question.

(3) A mark scheme showing the criteria for a grade-A response and for a grade-C response.

(4) Sample answers, most of which are grade A, B or C standard answers, although some are borderline cases. These are not model answers but rather a guide as to what standard of answer will attract the grades shown.

Democracy and representation

Question 1.1

(a) What do you understand by the term representative democracy? (5 marks)

(b) What is the role of a representative in the British parliament? (10 marks)

(c) Suggest three ways in which it could be argued that the British political system is undemocratic? (15 marks)

(d) In what ways can Britain be described as a liberal democracy? (20 marks)

Grade-A mark scheme for question 1.1 (65%+)

(a) An explanation of the basic nature of representative democracy is likely to be contrasted with direct democracy, with an explanation of why representative democracy is used rather than the direct form. The typical roles of representatives will be included. An example is likely to be used as an illustration, and the concept will be explained as fully as time reasonably allows.

(b) Answers should include explanations of the roles of members of parliament (MPs) and peers, though more attention is likely to be paid to MPs. The role of MPs as constituency representatives will be explained. This will be set against their role as party representatives and their attachment to a party manifesto. The fact that MPs call government to account will also be included. Answers may add further points such as interest group representation, MPs' relationship to the national interest and their limited role in the legislative process. Peers will be included in that they may represent various interests and may consider themselves as national representatives even though not elected.

(c) Three arguments must be described for a grade A and the arguments to pick from are: the unelected nature of the House of Lords; the nature of the first-past-the-post (FPTP) electoral system; the role and importance of the monarchy; the use of unrestrained prerogative powers; the lack of a written constitution and an entrenched bill of individual rights; the influence of quangos; and prime ministerial power. In each case, there must be a full description of the point and a clear explanation of why the feature can be considered undemocratic.

(d) Answers must reveal a clear knowledge of what a liberal democracy is likely to feature. Issues such as free elections, free opposition, the pluralist nature of the party system and the activities of pressure groups should be present. The rule of law is likely to be featured, as will the general respect for individual rights, limited government and civil equality. Most, though not all, of these points should be included with a clear explanation of what aspects of the British system conform to the criterion. Arguments that Britain is not a liberal democracy will not be credited.

Grade-A answer to question 1.1

(a) The idea of representative democracy was developed by the philosopher John Locke in the seventeenth century and put into practice by President James Madison in the US Constitution. It was used to replace absolute monarchy. The idea is that the people elect representatives whose job it is to check government and to be involved in the making of laws. These representatives may be removed if the people are dissatisfied. Representatives may use their own judgement (Burke's idea) or may act as strict delegates where they act directly in accordance with the wishes of the electorate. Any such system can be called a representative democracy.

e A grade-A response which is clear and accurate. Although the historical information is not necessary, it does give a good impression. The basic roles of representatives are included, though not illustrated from modern institutions. Normally, candidates would contrast representative democracy with direct democracy, but the quality of the response is generally good enough for this to be overlooked.

(b) The main representatives in the British system are MPs. They represent their constituencies, though mostly they are expected to represent their party and therefore the party manifesto. Some are also paid to represent interest groups in parliament and they speak on their behalf. Sometimes MPs may use their own judgement on some issues and sometimes they have a conflict of interests, e.g. between their party policy and the views of constituents. This may have happened to some over fox hunting recently. Members of the House of Lords are also sometimes representatives. They are members of important pressure groups and speak on behalf of powerful interests. Even though they are not elected, some peers believe they represent the whole nation.

e This answer is clearly expressed and well organised. It scrapes a grade A despite omitting the important work of MPs in the legislative process and in select and standing committees. However, the candidate has explained the conflicts of representation which occur and has also included the representative role of peers.

(c) I shall select three undemocratic parts of the British system and in each case explain why they are undemocratic.

Firstly, there is the House of Lords. This has a good deal of power as it is able to delay legislation, amend bills and can sometimes thwart the will of the elected majority in the House of Commons. None of the lords are elected. Most are appointed, though there are still some peers who owe their seat to an accident of birth. This is simply not democratic. The Lords is often called the 'biggest quango in town' or is accused of being full of 'Tony's cronies'.

Secondly, there is the role of the monarchy where the queen is not elected, unlike most democracies where the head of state is voted into office (e.g. France or the US). The monarch has huge potential powers, though most are carried out by the government. This is also undemocratic as the prerogative powers (on behalf of the monarch) are not democratically determined.

Finally, there is an electoral system which discriminates against small parties and means there are also many wasted votes in safe seats. It takes many more votes to elect a Liberal Democrat MP than MPs of larger parties. This makes votes unequal and is certainly not democratic. The idea of one-man-one-vote is destroyed by FPTP. Although the elections are generally free and fair, they are not fair to voters or candidates or parties. It means the House of Commons is not representative of the people in a democratic sense.

e A sound, grade-A answer. Each feature is accurately described and the answer retains complete focus on the question. Possibly there could be a little more development of the first two points, but there is enough for a top grade.

(d) Although there are many parts of the British system which are undemocratic as I have described in part (c) above, there are also many sides which conform to the idea of liberal democracy. I shall describe the main ones here and demonstrate why they are vital parts of a liberal democracy.

The term liberal implies freedom, and for the most part individual freedoms are respected in Britain. This is even more so now that the Human Rights Act has been passed. Parliament is still sovereign and can take away our rights, but Britain has a generally good human rights record. Liberalism also means free and fair elections and government by consent. Despite the unfair nature of the FPTP system, all legal parties and candidates may take part and everybody aged 18 or over is entitled to vote. There is freedom of expression and a free press so that everyone is fully informed.

Turning to government, we can see that it is properly elected and is accountable to the people through parliament. Parliament is a vital feature of a liberal democracy. The people are represented and government is responsible to them. Parliament also ensures that government obeys the rule of law. All laws must be properly passed through parliament and this makes laws legitimate and means they must be obeyed by all. We do not have the separation of powers, but the judiciary is independent and free of political control for the most part.

Everybody is equal under the law in Britain, according to A.V. Dicey's well-known rule of law. This is enforced by the judiciary and by parliament. All acts of government must be carried out in accordance with the laws.

So, although Britain has some undemocratic aspects and is not a perfect liberal democracy, there are a number of ways in which the nation is a true liberal democracy.

e Another solid, grade-A answer. There are no major aspects which are omitted and the candidate has not fallen into the trap of putting the other side of the argument when it is not required.

e **The answers gain most of the marks available for clear expression and quality of writing. The candidate might lose some analysis and evaluation marks for not developing certain points quite fully enough, but gains many marks for focusing**

clearly on the questions. Most of the marks for knowledge are awarded as the range of points used is always relevant and the answers are comprehensive within the tight time limits. Overall, this is a good grade-A response.

■ ■ ■

Grade-C answer to question 1.1

(a) There are two types of democracy: direct democracy and representative democracy. Direct democracy is where the people make all the important decisions directly. The problem with this is that the people do not always know best and may be swayed by emotional speakers and the tabloid press. To avoid this we can elect representatives who can make decisions on our behalf. Burke said that they should use their judgement, but today they mostly follow the party line. So it is a kind of indirect democracy.

e The candidate has approached the question in an indirect way, and fails to describe the various roles of representatives. There is some development using the Burke analysis, but the answer should refer to legislation and calling government to account. This is a borderline B or C response that, while accurate, does not develop the ideas enough.

(b) British MPs have a number of roles to play. They have a part in the legislating process, although they mostly obey the commands of the party whips. An MP also has the job of bringing the government to accountability by asking questions in parliament. In some cases, MPs vote no confidence in a government which will cause an election. MPs also represent their constituents, again by asking parliamentary questions. A few sit in committees which may amend legislation and ask questions of ministers and civil servants. Some MPs are also sponsored, for example by trade unions. They lobby ministers for them and may ask questions. We are now using referendums and this is undermining the work of representatives.

MPs are members of their political party and some of them see this as their main function. They may simply become lobby fodder by obeying the whips and ignoring the wishes of constituents. In this way they are not acting as true representatives.

e The student has produced quite a full answer, but loses marks in two main areas. The first is in omitting to mention peers in a question that stipulates a consideration of parliament and not just the House of Commons. Secondly, the answer is not always well expressed and mixes up the work of MPs in committees and, in particular, is confused in describing the role of representatives in making government accountable. Reference to this point is not made clearly enough. This is a grade-C answer.

(c) Firstly there is the electoral system which is completely unfair. The small parties get a bad deal and the voters have to vote tactically (not for their first choice but their second choice in case their vote is wasted). The parties with concentrated support will do better than those with scattered support. This is unequal and unfair. It means that governments are elected with a minority of support. In fact, nearly every MP does not win 50% of the vote.

There is also the problem that the party leaders completely dominate parliament. As we have already seen above, MPs do not think for themselves and usually ignore the wishes of their constituents. They are just lobby fodder. This means that government can get legislation through the Commons without proper consideration. This is not democratic. There is no chance that a government will lose a vote if it has a large majority, even if a bill does not have the support of the public. In addition, the prime minister dominates the parties and some say we have prime ministerial government. Lord Hailsham called this 'elective dictatorship'.

Thirdly we should consider the House of Lords. This body is not elected and yet it plays an important role in making and amending laws. This is outrageously undemocratic. It has been made more democratic by removing hereditary peers but there are still many in place and the rest are merely appointed. Members of the Lords are not representative in that they are mostly old, all men and do not represent ethnic groups and different religions. The monarchy is associated with the House of Lords and this is also not democratic. It is not elected and yet it has a great deal of power.

e A full answer, though arguably it contains five features and credit can only be given for three. The comments on elective dictatorship (wrongly ascribed to the power of the prime minister) and on the monarchy are separate points, though the candidate does not treat them as such. It is also problematic to suggest that the power of party whips is undemocratic because attachment to the manifesto can be seen as democratic. A minor error suggests that there are only men in the Lords. Otherwise the candidate loses out through a lack of development of the valid points. The monarchy or prime ministerial government needed a fuller treatment instead of being added in as afterthoughts. There is enough accurate information for a grade C.

(d) A liberal democracy contains the following features: elections are held fairly and everybody is entitled to take part; there are basic freedoms such as freedom of expression, movement, thought, religion and association; it must be representative in that the legislature is properly elected; in some cases there should be referenda so that the people can decide key questions; government must be accountable to the people and there should be government by consent; there should also be a proper constitution which controls the government and regulates the rights of citizens. The question is, does Britain conform to this?

Well, first we do have free elections, though the electoral system is probably not democratic enough. All parties can take part and everyone can vote or form a political party. Our rights are mostly protected but we do not have a Bill of Rights as the US does. The Human Rights Act has incorporated the European Convention on Human Rights so British citizens can now go to court to enforce their rights. But there have been many cases where police powers have been increased and there is little to stop a government taking away our rights.

Parliament is free, although the MPs are dominated by the party whips and the prime minister. Government is accountable to parliament, but when did you last hear of a government being voted down by MPs? And ministers do not resign even when they are criticised by parliament. We also do not have a written constitution so that we do not know our rights. Instead, parliament is sovereign and cannot be controlled except at elections.

e The candidate has made a major mistake. The question only asks for aspects which conform to liberal democracy but the answer discusses whether or not Britain is a liberal democracy. Much of the discussion is unnecessary and so gets no credit. However, there is a sound description of liberal democracy and, while ignoring mention of pluralism, the answer identifies a few positive aspects of the British democracy. The student should be clearer about what can be said to be democratic and what cannot. This is just about a grade-C response.

e **Overall the candidate receives a grade C for answers which, while essentially sound, suffer from a number of problems: lack of focus on the questions; lack of development of key points; and some muddled explanations which look like the result of weak revision and a fault in the division of time. The answer for part (c) is slightly fuller than for part (d) even though the latter carries more marks, so the candidate may have had to rush the final part.**

Question 1.2

Study the following data:

Referendum results on Scottish devolution, 11 September 1997

Question	% in favour	% against
Do you want a Scottish parliament established?	74.3	25.7
Do you want a Scottish parliament to have tax-varying powers?	63.5	36.5

Turnout: 61.5% of the total electorate

Referendum result on Welsh devolution, 11 September 1997

Question	% in favour	% against
Do you want a devolved government and assembly	50.3	49.7

Turnout: 51.2% of the total electorate

(a) What do the results of the referenda shown indicate about the purposes of referenda? (12 marks)

(b) What evidence is there to suggest that the Scottish referendum was a successful exercise in democracy, but the Welsh vote was not? (20 marks)

(c) What additional arguments can be suggested against the use of referenda to resolve important political issues? (28 marks)

(d) Explain the reasons in favour of the wider use of referenda in Britain. (30 marks)

Grade-A mark scheme for question 1.2 (65%+)

(a) Answers must identify all the issues at stake to include both decisions on devolved government and, in the case of Scotland, whether taxation could be varied by a Scottish parliament. There should then be conclusions drawn about types of issues. Candidates must identify important constitutional change — the devolution of power and taxation powers are the examples — as the main reason for referenda. It should be pointed out that such changes require the clear consent of the people. The point that referenda entrench such constitutional changes may be included, and the question of whether decisions are legitimate should definitely be mentioned.

(b) The main evidence identified will be the turnout at the two referenda and the size of the majority in each case. Strong responses will point to the high Scottish turnout and big 'yes' majority as evidence of success but will point out that even this did not represent an overall majority of the electorate. The same analysis should be applied to the question on taxation powers. The two problems with the Welsh vote were low turnout and the narrowness of the majority. Good responses must point out that this may be seen as failure because there is lack of clear consent for change.

(c) A full discussion of all or most of the issues. Evidence contained in part (b) need not be repeated as the question says 'additional'. The points raised will be all or most of the following, with appropriate examples used: the complexity of issues (single European currency); the fact that the majority may use such votes to oppress minorities as in Northern Ireland; the possibility of emotional, not rational, responses (the death penalty); the undue influence of wealthy minorities (e.g. James Goldsmith on membership of the European Union [EU]); the undermining of the authority of elected representatives (e.g. devolution); the fact that referenda will entrench change so that flexibility is lost (e.g. electoral reform); and the influence of tabloid newspapers. Any other cogent arguments will be accepted, if properly framed and illustrated.

(d) A full range of the issues should be developed with appropriate examples. The range is likely to include: the need to obtain the consent of the people (develop the theme in, perhaps, Northern Ireland or over Scottish taxation powers); the concept that important constitutional change should not be in the hands of a temporary majority in parliament and government (single currency); the need to entrench constitutional change to protect it from reversal by future governments (electoral reform); and as a solution for a government which is split on an issue (the 1975 EU referendum, EU issues). Strong responses may also refer to the increasing technical ability to use referenda (for example, via the internet) and are likely to refer to the concept of direct democracy.

Grade-A answer to question 1.2

(a) These referenda were about devolution of power to Scotland and Wales and the question about tax-varying power for the Scottish parliament. There was also a referendum over devolution and the Good Friday Agreement in Northern Ireland. Why were they held? The answer is that these were important constitutional changes and the Labour government believed that these changes needed the clear consent of the people. The issue about tax was possibly the most important as people must consent to being taxed, which is an ancient principle. The principle has now been established that changes in the way people are governed will be put to a vote. This will also apply to the question of the euro and maybe to electoral reform.

e This answer is just about as good as it can get. The candidate is clearly well read on the issue and writes well in a response that has looked beyond the bare facts of the data to consider the wider issues suggested. This is a high grade-A response.

(b) At first sight it may appear that the Scottish votes were a success and the Welsh votes were not. There was a higher turnout in Scotland and both votes there showed a clear majority. There was surely overwhelming consent for change in Scotland. The narrow Welsh 'yes' vote combined with a low turnout meant that only about a quarter of the Welsh people actively wanted devolution.

We should look further. At least there was a majority in Wales — and it would have embarrassed the government if they had voted 'no'. So the government had its way. The low turnout is important, but everybody had a chance to vote. It was in one sense a success. On the other hand, the Scottish vote is not so clear. If you calculate the results, most Scots either voted 'no' or simply stayed at home. So, no great enthusiasm. This is even more important with the vote about taxation.

On balance, we can say that the Welsh vote was something of a failure and the Scottish vote a success but that there are arguments suggesting the opposite in both cases.

e Another exceptional response with all aspects covered in a clear writing style. Above all, the student goes beyond the obvious answer to examine the issues critically and to reveal how both sides of the votes could be analysed.

(c) Although the idea of direct votes on key issues seems a great idea, there are many arguments which can be made against their use. I shall examine these in this section, but will describe the positive arguments in section (d).

Devolution was possibly quite an easy issue to understand, but this is not always true. Some questions are very difficult to understand. Let's take the issue of introducing proportional representation in British elections. Everyone can understand why some systems are fairer than others, but it is very difficult for people to see the arguments about the political effects of reform. What about coalitions or minorities? What about allowing small parties into government? People find these questions difficult, so it is not fair to ask them to give an opinion. Furthermore, people who do not know any better might be influenced by tabloid journalists or by a rich businessman like James Goldsmith over complicated issues. This is not healthy in a democracy.

It is often said that we should have a vote on the death penalty. This shows up another argument against referendums. People will vote with their hearts and not their heads. Suppose, just before the referendum, there was a gruesome child murder or an abuse case. People would obviously vote for the death penalty. On another day they may hear about a person who was wrongly hanged like the convict in Texas who was executed with a mental age of nine. The vote would be the other way round.

The main argument is that having elected a parliament and a government, what is the point of then voting on issues ourselves? 'Why get a dog and then bark yourself?' some people say. Referenda will undermine the authority of government and we will soon have votes on everything. This will lead to voter apathy and low turnouts will result.

Having examined these arguments against referenda, I will look at the other arguments in section (d).

e Another grade-A response in which the quality of analysis is high. The candidate loses some marks for content by omitting a few points, but, on the whole, has prepared well for the exam and been able to put forward ideas and give examples.

(d) There are many strong arguments in favour of more use of referenda and I shall examine these in turn.

Most important is the idea of government by consent which is a vital part of liberal democracy. When important changes are afoot — like devolution or the introduction of the euro — it is important that people have their say. There is an elected government, but elections may be a long way off. In addition, people do not vote for governments on any particular issue. The only way to gauge widespread support is by having a referendum on an issue.

Important constitutional changes, such as the Good Friday Agreement, will last for many years, so the people must be involved. A government may only be in power for 4 or 5 years, but these changes may last for generations. It was vital to get public support for this controversial change.

There have been times when the government cannot decide an issue, as happened in 1975 over membership of the European Community. A vote was needed then because otherwise the government might have collapsed. Ministers were freed of collective responsibility and campaigned both ways. So referenda may get government out of a mess.

Running out of time...will finish with bullet points.

- will guard changes against being repealed by future governments (proportional representation (PR))
- e-democracy and internet can be used for inexpensive and fast results
- people are better informed these days
- conclusion: referenda are growing in popularity and are likely to be used more in future

e This near-perfect performance lapses as the candidate runs out of time due to earlier over-long answers. However, the student has done the right thing by ending with bullet points rather than coming to an abrupt halt and has salvaged most of the content marks. Some marks are lost for weak expression and the bullet points lack the development to secure all the analysis marks. This response would merit a low A.

e **The candidate is clearly an excellent student who is awarded a high grade A. Most cannot aspire to the quality of the writing or the level of background knowledge, but all can learn from the approach. The student has read a great deal and prepared key (and predictable) topics by learning a number of points and examples. Each point is developed fully and, where possible, analysed from more than one point of view. Although time ran out, this was not critical because of the quality of the previous work. However, it is important to keep an eye on the time.**

Grade-C answer to question 1.2

(a) These were votes about devolution. This was a proposal to devolve power to a Welsh Assembly and a Scottish Parliament. It was also about transferring taxation powers to Scotland. A referendum is a system for asking all the people in a country about an important question instead of government making the decision.

e The student has taken the question at face value and has failed to address the general issue of what sort of policy might be the subject of a referendum. Good answers should use the data and then try to look beyond them to the wider questions they raise. The candidate has identified correctly the purpose of these referenda and knows what a referendum is, but displays no wider knowledge. This is a D-grade response.

(b) The Welsh referendum was not successful because there was a low turnout (51.2%). There was a much better turnout in Scotland (61.5 %). This means the Welsh were not very interested. It was a failure because the government did not get the Welsh interested and the Welsh majority was very small. So only about one quarter of the Welsh people actually wanted devolution. This was a failure because the Welsh were given a change which they did not really want. The Scottish vote was better as most of the Scots clearly wanted devolution and tax powers and that is what they got.

e This is a borderline C/D grade because the candidate has not addressed all aspects of the data. The vote on taxation powers, which was different from the main Scottish vote, has been largely ignored, as has the issue of legitimacy in the voting. The student is also uncritical of the Scottish vote, not seeing that it could be questioned as a success. However, several key points are identified, notably turnout, which is enough to earn some marks.

(c) The main argument about referenda is that you are likely to get low turnouts, as occurred in the Welsh vote. Also, there may not be a very large majority so nothing is achieved. Some issues are much too difficult for people to understand and they may be influenced by the tabloid newspapers' lurid headlines. The imminent question about the euro is a good example. People do not understand the economic arguments but are influenced by those who argue about the queen's head on the pound and things like that. It is better if people who understand the issues, like ministers and civil servants, make these decisions and the people can vote them out of power if they wish. Referenda are also slow and expensive ways of making decisions.

Many people say we should have a referendum on the death penalty and the result would be that we would bring it back. This would not be a good decision as so many mistakes are made as we see in the US. But people would vote for it because of the publicity about child abuse and terrorism and so on. This is not a good reason, and people say that 'wise heads should prevail'.

So for these and many other reasons we should not use referendums except in exceptional circumstances.

e The student has made three or four valid points and explained them quite well with appropriate examples. There is a decent grasp of the concept of the electoral mandate when discussing the role of ministers and the electorate and this helps to obtain a grade C. The answer does not achieve more because it leaves out some important points (see the A-grade mark scheme). The candidate has also included unnecessary material at the beginning, referring to issues from section (b). The answer is not well organised and the powers of expression are not very strong. The style is also a little too casual. The candidate gets just over half the marks for powers of expression, content and analysis.

(d) There are many reasons why referenda are a good idea in spite of the arguments against, shown in section (c).

Firstly, there is the idea of direct democracy which was developed by Plato in Athens. Here all the people (excluding slaves and women) made political decisions for themselves. This perfect democracy is the ideal situation and perhaps one to follow because it is not always true that the 'government knows best'. The people should decide matters that affect them.

Secondly, it is important that people have a say in decisions they will have to obey. If the British people are not asked about the euro, they may not wish to use it and there will be complete chaos. The same is true of devolution (see data). It is important that people want a major change instead of just forcing them into it. The Scottish people wanted a parliament, so they got one.

Thirdly, there are often cases when the government cannot make up its own mind about an issue. This happened in 1975 when the Labour government was split over Europe and Harold Wilson called a referendum (a 65% 'yes' vote) to solve the problem. Britain stayed in Europe successfully and the same sort of result may happen again over the euro where, once again, there is not a solid consensus within government. The electoral reform debate is also divided equally in New Labour, so what better way than to put it to the people?

We can see that there are three main reasons why referenda are a good idea and these probably outweigh the arguments against.

e This is a better section and worth a grade B. The candidate was clearly better prepared and this showed in the quality of writing. Although one or two key points are omitted, three strong points are chosen (though the reference to Plato is wrong because he was opposed to direct democracy). The candidate understands the concept of legitimacy and consent, although no direct references are made to these concepts. In other words, the student shows *implicit* rather than *explicit* understanding of the concept to earn most of the marks for that aspect of analysis. A clearer statement about legitimacy would be necessary for a grade A.

e **Overall, this is a grade-C response, pulled up by a strong section (d), which carries most marks. The candidate needed to be better prepared; key points were omitted, especially in section (c). In the first sections the candidate did not respond fully enough to all the data shown. Where the preparation was sound, so was the writing quality.**

Question 1.3

Read the following passage:

Since 1997 the British seem to have developed a taste for the use of referenda, which had previously been considered a peculiarity of continental Europeans. In Britain, respect for our representative institutions — mainly government and parliament — prevented us from considering the possibility that the people might be allowed to resolve important issues. There was also a fear that the mass of people was simply incapable of understanding complex political issues. This rather conservative and paternalistic attitude was held in common by both the Labour Party and the Conservative Party itself. The first full-scale referendum took place in 1975 to decide whether Britain should remain a member of the European Community. However, it was seen as a one-off exercise, designed to get the government out of a political mess because the Labour cabinet of the day was split on the issue. By asking the people, the cabinet was able to resolve its internal dispute. For the next 20 years, the idea of using referenda was largely forgotten except among Liberal politicians. More recently, however, referenda are once again in vogue. Several have already been held and it seems there are more to come. This is partly a reflection of declining respect for politicians, but may also have a great deal to do with the new appetite for constitutional change.

Original material

(a) Identify and explain the arguments against the use of referenda which are mentioned in the passage. (6 marks)

(b) Describe and explain the use of referenda in Britain since 1975. (12 marks)

(c) Using information in the passage and your own knowledge, construct an argument in favour of the greater future use of referenda in Britain. (22 marks)

Grade-A mark scheme for question 1.3 (65%+)

(a) All aspects referred to in the passage will be identified and explained. These are: the belief that we should respect our elected representatives and referenda might undermine this; the paternalistic idea that people are not capable of deciding issues for themselves; the notion that referenda are a continental peculiarity, with the passage suggesting that the British saw themselves as superior in these matters to other Europeans.

(b) Mention should be made of all British referenda, though it may be acceptable if the referendum in Northern Ireland in the 1970s or the London mayoral election are omitted. The 1975 referendum on Europe should be quoted along with reasons why it was held. The failed votes on devolution for Scotland and Wales in 1978 should be described. They were needed because it was far from clear that the policy enjoyed widespread support. The devolution votes of the 1990s should be described, with comments that they were constitutional changes that needed popular consent. The Northern Ireland vote should be picked out as crucial in view of the divided nature of Ulster society and the need for consensus. The vote on an elected London mayor was a political change needing the consent of the London people, especially as it had taxation implications. The strongest candidates will refer to local referenda on Sunday pub opening in Wales and on expenditure plans by various authorities. Reasonably full explanations of each point will be required.

(c) Reference must be made to the government split in 1975, the low respect for elected politicians and the prevalence of recent constitutional changes. The issue of constitutional change should be fully explained, referring to the need for legitimacy and the need to entrench constitutional change. Examples should be added, such as electoral reform and the introduction of the euro. References should be made to the concept of direct democracy. It should be pointed out that people are better educated and informed and so are able to judge issues more clearly. There is also better technology available for referenda, notably the internet. Best answers might refer to the greater hunger for direct democracy and the perceived need for government to serve the needs of the public directly. Any other cogent reasons, properly argued and developed, will be credited.

■ ■ ■

Borderline grade-A/B answer to question 1.3

(a) There are two arguments in the passage. The first is that referenda will reduce our respect for government and parliament because they have been elected to make decisions on our behalf. The second is that people cannot understand complicated issues and so cannot make their own decisions. The passage describes this as a 'conservative' idea.

e The student has correctly identified the two main points and explained them to a grade-B standard. An A grade would have referred to what was happening in Europe and to the implied sense of British insularity or superiority. The candidate should have looked at the whole passage and referred to what is relevant.

(b) The passage refers to the 1975 referendum which had to happen because the government could not make up its mind on the issue. The other main referenda were the ones to decide about devolution in Scotland, Wales and Northern Ireland in 1997 and 1998. These had to happen because it was necessary to discover whether the Scottish and Welsh people consented to the change. They had voted against devolution in the 1970s so a second vote was clearly needed.

There was a vote on whether London should have an elected mayor. The government was not sure about this — perhaps it hoped for a 'no' vote and so held a referendum in London. There was a huge 'yes' vote. There are likely to be more such votes in other cities. Some local authorities have held votes on the level of council tax and how to spend money in their districts. These are kinds of local referenda.

e The candidate has missed out the crucial referendum on the Good Friday Agreement in Ulster and the Republic of Ireland, a serious omission since it opens up some important principles. The answer compensates somewhat by including local referenda, but the development of the reasons behind the devolution votes is rather weak. The reasons given for the vote on the elected London mayor are shaky and should have been balanced against the official reason given. This is a borderline C/D grade and reveals a student who should have been better prepared.

(c) There are many reasons why the use of referenda is a good idea. I will explain these and conclude by giving an assessment of whether referenda should be used in future.

Referenda are known as direct democracy, which has its origins in ancient Greece. Then a well-educated portion of the population was considered capable of making important decisions. It is an open question whether the British people are educated enough, but we do have freedom of information and everyone can watch television and read newspapers. Perhaps they can make important decisions.

Apart from devolution (which is described above), we have several important issues to come. There is the single European currency, the change to a different electoral system and we may have votes on membership of the EU. It may even be that Scotland and Wales will want independence in the future. These are important changes and it is vital that the people have their say. It is not satisfactory or democratic enough for these issues to be decided by parliament, especially as government dominates parliament. John Stuart Mill said we should have government by consent, and referenda will provide this.

We know that parliament is weak and that people are more interested in pressure groups and opinion polls and making their views known in phone-in programmes etc. So in our modern pluralist society we need a new decision-making system which involves people more directly. Referenda involve everybody — individuals, the media, the press and pressure groups as well as MPs and ministers.

Finally, I would point out that Britain has a flexible constitution which is easy to change. Perhaps it is too flexible and we have an elective dictatorship (Lord Hailsham), so government can make changes on a whim. By having referenda on issues like the single currency and a new election system, we can put the constitution under the control of the people — where it belongs.

On balance — despite the problems mentioned in the extract above — it seems that referenda are a good thing in a modern democracy. They involve people and protect us from over-powerful government. In a modern pluralist society we need more such votes, not fewer.

e Although the candidate has omitted a few important arguments, the best has been saved for part (c) where most of the marks are concentrated. Some content marks are lost, but this is offset by high marks for the quality of analysis and powers of expression. The writing on pluralism and constitutional change is well prepared. The final paragraph was not needed as only *one* side of the argument was requested. No marks are lost, but a little time was wasted. This last section is worth a grade A.

e **Overall, the candidate is on the borderline between a grade B and an A. Had revision coverage been more complete and the response to section (a) more thorough, then a low or middle grade A would have been assured. Fortunately, the candidate balanced the time well and saved the biggest effort for where most of the marks lay.**

Topic 2

Elections, electoral reform and voting behaviour

Question 2.1

Read the following passage:

The 1997 general election was an example, *par excellence*, of a dealigned election. The underpinnings of aligned voting — class and party identification — were weaker than ever. Evaluations of party leaders and the performance of the government in general were the main influences on voters, overriding even the improving economy in the run-up to the election. The consequence was a huge overturn of votes.

Perhaps surprisingly, this conclusion offers a message of hope for the Conservatives. With a dealigned electorate the electoral tide that swept them away could, given the right combination of circumstances, flow back in their direction just as rapidly.

Source: 'Dealignment vindicated', David Denver, *Politics Review*, Vol. 9, No. 4, 2000.

(a) What does the article suggest were the main factors in the outcome of the 1997 general election? (6 marks)

(b) What is meant by dealignment and why is it such an important feature of modern voting behaviour? (12 marks)

(c) What were the main factors which influenced the outcome of the 2001 general election? (22 marks)

Grade-A mark scheme for question 2.1 (65%+)

(a) This answer must identify the two main factors influencing the 1997 election as government performance and opinions about the party leaders. Answers should also mention the fact that economic performance must have been influential, but that the other two factors were more important. There is no requirement to mention class voting.

(b) The term dealignment must be split into its two meanings of class and partisan dealignment. Class dealignment should be explained as the general fragmentation of the traditional class system and the fact that people no longer place themselves clearly in a class structure. The effect of this on class-based voting should be described. Partisan dealignment refers to looser party identification and candidates must give some reasons why this is happening.

(c) This should be a full description of several factors, though some will be omitted owing to time constraints. In each case, the factor will be accurately described and there will be full development of the point. Any point will be accepted as valid provided it is underpinned by evidence or sound argument. The question refers to 'main factors', so more credit will be given to major than to minor factors.

■ ■ ■

Grade-A answer to question 2.1

(a) The article clearly states that although we would have expected the economic situation to have determined the result and things were improving ('It's the economy, stupid,' said Bill Clinton before the 1992 US election), other factors were important. These were the performance of the party leaders, where Tony Blair looked much more effective than the sitting prime minister, John Major, who could not keep his cabinet together. The other factor was the performance of the Conservative government. There was a great deal of sleaze and the government was split over Europe. Labour was determined and united and had a 'squeaky clean' look.

> e This is a grade-A response which deserves full marks because it is accurate, well expressed, fully developed and goes a little beyond the sample text.

(b) The term dealignment appeared in the 1970s as an explanation for changing voting behaviour. Heath, Jowell and Curtice and others pointed out that class had been the dominant factor in voting behaviour. This meant that most people had a strong party allegiance, based on their class (often self-assigned). Crewe and others pointed out that the class system began to break down in the 1970s. This had two effects. The first was known as class dealignment. People no longer fitted into a neat class system. Many members of the working class were becoming affluent with middle-class life styles, buying cars, foreign holidays and their homes. The middle class was also breaking up into various groups such as management, entrepreneurs and the caring professions. This made it more difficult to predict how people would vote.

Partisan dealignment was the other change. Before the 1970s, most people identified closely with one party and always voted for it. Very few people were 'floating voters'. This partisanship has weakened, mainly because of class dealignment. This means that voting is more volatile and based on instrumental (self-interest) factors.

These are the two types of dealignment mentioned in the passage. They are the main factors in current voting behaviour.

> e Another excellent A grade for an accurate and well-written answer that develops its points and shows a wide knowledge. The candidate had clearly revised the topic thoroughly and had a response planned.

(c) Although the factors mentioned in the article were still present at the 2001 election, it is interesting that Denver says there was some hope for the Conservatives. In fact, the Conservatives did virtually as badly in 2001 as they did in 1997. I shall look first at the factors mentioned by Denver and then examine some other issues which have come to light since the election.

First, we have evaluation of the leaders. There is no doubt that the press and the media damaged William Hague. He was seen as a figure of fun. The fact that he was 'bald and spoke with a funny accent' was always being referred to. Blair was also criticised, but this was for being too strong rather than too weak. I believe that Blair won the battle of the leaderships, although the man who came out best was Charles Kennedy, which may explain the Liberal Democrats' strong showing.

Next, we have the performance of the parties. People still apparently remembered the mistakes made by the Tories before 1997. By contrast, Labour had quite a good record with a stable economy and some improvements in education and law and order. The electorate was obviously worried about the lack of progress in health, but there were many other popular policies such as the minimum wage, interest rates being decided by the Bank of England, devolution and so on. The Conservatives did not seem to have alternatives.

There were other factors too. The economy was the most important. People feel secure with low inflation, unemployment and interest rates. Bill Clinton in the USA said 'it's the economy, stupid' when asked what won elections for him. This was also true for Labour. People contrast this with the recession under John Major and the ERM fiasco.

It is also true that Labour is a very united party whereas the Conservatives continue to tear themselves apart over Europe. They tried to make Europe the central issue, but the electorate consider health, education and law and order the more important issues. They trust Labour more than the Conservatives on these themes. Voters do not like divided parties and the Conservatives therefore suffered badly.

Some of the other less important factors seem to be as follows. First, there was tactical voting against the Conservatives. This helped the Liberal Democrats gain some ground. Then there was the media, most of which put its weight behind Labour. It is not known how much influence the press has, but it is true that most papers supported Labour including the *Sun*, the *Mirror* and even the Tory *Daily Express*.

I would also identify the fact that there were concerns over some of the leading Conservatives such as Portillo and Widdecombe who are not popular.

So, overall, it seems that the same factors which won Labour the election in 1997 worked again in 2001. There was unhappiness about Labour's performance, but not enough for large numbers to change their votes. Labour has captured the centre ground and that is where most of the voters are. As Denver says, class is no longer very important in voting, so the class image of the party matters less than its policies and performance. The real winners were the Liberal Democrats who strengthened their position and showed that 1997 was not a flash in the pan.

e This is a strong A-grade answer, a comprehensive, well-expressed review. It refers to the stimulus well, but goes considerably beyond it. It ranges widely, including the Liberal Democrats and not just the two main parties. The candidate also does a good job of comparing 1997 with 2001. The answer is critically strong, distinguishing between issues which are important and those which may be minor. There is some speculation, but as it was written soon after the 2001 election, this is inevitable. The great strength of this answer is that the candidate is well informed about current events. This is essential when discussing political events rather than theories.

The student has read a great deal on this subject, writes well and has delivered a grade-A response as a result of being properly prepared.

■ ■ ■

Grade-B answer to question 2.1

(a) There are two factors mentioned in the passage. The first is the party leaderships. The party leaders are important in deciding how people are likely to vote. If they are powerful and charismatic, they will win votes. The other factor is the government as a whole. Obviously, people will judge the government and decide against the performance of the opposition.

This student has correctly identified the two most important factors but has failed to expand on them enough and has not referred to economic factors.

(b) Dealignment is an important factor in modern voting behaviour. It used to be true that most people voted for the same party, usually the same as their parents. Working-class people obviously tended to support Labour and the middle classes voted Conservative and occasionally Liberal. This is because they believed the parties looked after their class. All this has changed.

People do not support the same party all their lives, partly because the parties have changed and partly because of instrumental voting — an idea developed by Ivor Crewe. People vote selfishly and look at the issues which affect them. So home-owners tend to vote Tory whereas the poor vote Labour because they think there will be more benefits for them. This is known as dealignment. There are more floating voters and people vote differently at each election. Some vote one way in a general election and another way in local elections.

The passage clearly says that dealignment was a cause of the landslide against the Tories and it could bring them back in again. This is what he means by the tide turning. No party can be sure of its votes any more because, as the passage says, people will change support according to issues, the party leaders and the performance of the government as a whole.

The candidate clearly knows what dealignment means and has expanded on it well enough for a grade C. The failure is in not spotting that class and party are the two aspects of dealignment. There is a generalised sense of this in the answer but the candidate needs to describe each clearly and show how they are connected. The quality of writing is variable, and the candidate is inadequately prepared for a predictable question.

(c) The 2001 election showed an almost identical result to 1997. This means that the same factors were operating in both elections. I shall look at these factors in turn.

First, there is the leadership issue. Hague is unpopular, although he has done well at question time. People do not like the way he looks or speaks. He seems very out of touch and is a generally weak leader. Tony Blair is something of a control freak but most people trust him even if they do not like him. He won the leadership battle, and it is my view that this was the main factor in this election.

Then there was the tabloid press which has a great role in determining which party people support. The *Sun* backed Labour again and most of the papers did the same. They said 'let's give Labour one more chance' and the people agreed. Papers influence how many people vote and there is no doubt they did so in 1992, 1997 and 2001.

Next we come to the question of the economy. There is no doubt that everybody trusts Gordon Brown. He has made the right decisions and has been very careful with the British economy. He has kept a tight rein on spending and has kept taxes down. There has been low inflation, the minimum wage and interest rates are down, thanks to handing over control to the Bank of England. The Conservatives do not have different economic policies except to stay out of the euro, which will be the subject of a referendum in the future anyway.

The Conservatives concentrated on Europe and asylum seekers which did not interest the public as much as health, education and transport. Labour had the edge in these policy areas. It has to be said that the low turnout (under 60%) was partly because many people did not like the policies of either party very much but were prepared to give Labour another chance. People were also unhappy about the Conservatives playing the race card when they had signed a declaration to keep race out of the election.

In conclusion, I would identify the state of the economy, the better leadership qualities of Blair and his frontbench team, and the influence of the tabloid press as the main factors in the result of the 2001 election. It was very similar to 1997 and most of the same factors were important.

e This candidate has identified some key features. However, this is a C-grade response for a number of reasons. First, it is not comprehensive enough. Several issues are omitted, including tactical voting, the divisions in the Conservative leadership and the performance of the Liberal Democrats. Second, its evaluation is a little weak. Some attempt is made to identify the more important issues, but many minor ones are omitted. The question of press influence is put simply and does not admit any doubt about its influence. Finally, it is not very well written and is clumsy in places. It is a solid answer showing some good knowledge and understanding, but does not go beyond those qualities.

The candidate had the knowledge to obtain a comfortable B grade instead of low grade C. Better planning and organisation could have put matters right without too much effort.

Question 2.2

(a) Describe Britain's first-past-the-post (FPTP) electoral system. (5 marks)

(b) Describe any one other electoral system used for elections in Britain. (10 marks)

(c) Why does the FPTP system favour some parties and not others? (15 marks)

(d) What are the main political results of using the FPTP system? (20 marks)

Grade-A mark scheme for question 2.2 (65%+)

(a) There should be a clear description of how FPTP works, explaining how a plurality is required for winning the seat. It should be made clear that this is not the same as needing an overall majority. The fact that each voter has only one vote should be stated. The effects within constituencies should be described but there is no credit for effects on parties as a whole as this is part of section (c). Evaluation of the system is not required.

(b) A description of the additional member system (AMS) or the single transferable vote (STV) or the regional list system is required. It might be permissible to describe the system for electing the London mayor. The system must be clearly and accurately described and its effects shown with reference to how the elections turned out. There should be as much detail and development as the limited time allows.

(c) The main point must be fully described: that parties with concentrated support have an advantage over those whose support is dispersed. The effects on specific parties should be described. The differential value of voting may be referred to, as may the likelihood of tactical voting.

(d) There will be a complete description of why the system tends to result in decisive victories by a single party. The effects of single-party government should be explained, referring to such features as executive dominance of the legislature, the absence of coalitions, the strength of the mandate and manifesto system. Each point will be fully developed.

Grade-A answer to question 2.2

(a) Britain's system is known as a plurality system in single member constituencies. This means that in each constituency it is the candidate who wins the largest number of votes who wins. He or she does not need an overall majority of 50% plus and it is quite possible to win a seat with only a third of the votes. Indeed, most MPs do not enjoy an overall majority. Voters only have one vote. They cannot choose between candidates from one party and their second or third choices are not included. So there is one vote and the winner takes all.

e This is a clear grade-A response in which all the criteria are met.

(b) I shall describe the STV system, which has been adopted for assembly and local elections in Northern Ireland. It is being used because it is a particularly proportional system that aims to achieve a consensus in Northern Ireland and to support the Good Friday Agreement by having all Ulster parties represented.

There are multi-member constituencies and voters can vote for all the candidates from any party. They place the candidates in order of preference and can vote for more than one party. Every candidate must achieve a quota which is a proportion of the vote calculated by a complicated formula. Second, third and further preference votes are added up until the required number of candidates has the quota. The purpose is to make the result proportional, to give voters more choice and to give more parties a chance to win seats. The result is that many parties have won seats in the Northern Ireland Assembly. Sinn Fein did well because of the system and therefore has a share in government.

It also means that each constituency has more than one member and so people can be represented by a member of the party for which they voted. This gives more choice to voters.

e A high grade-A answer, which concentrates on key points. The candidate was clearly well prepared to explain the system and did so effectively, developing the effects of the system without wasting time on marginal points.

(c) The FPTP is better for some parties, mainly the big ones. However, it should be said that the Conservatives suffered in Scotland and Wales, and in 1997 won no seats in either country. So it is not just big parties which gain. The real picture is that parties do well under FPTP if they have concentrated support in some regions. It is possible to win seats with about 40% of the vote, but if your support is spread out among many constituencies this is very difficult. The Liberal Democrats are the main losers as they often win 20–30% of the vote in constituencies in some regions, but this is not enough. The Liberal Democrats do have concentrated support in parts of Scotland and the southwest of England and win seats there. The Greens and other very small parties do badly because they have small support that is highly dispersed.

There are small parties which can do well, such as Plaid Cymru and the Scottish Nationalist Party (SNP). This is because they have pockets of concentrated support. So it is not just large parties which gain but those which have concentrated support. Labour does best because it has a lot of support in urban areas where most people live. The Conservatives do well in the south for the same reason, but in Scotland and Wales their 20% or so support is evenly spread. They did much better in the devolution elections which used proportional representation (PR).

e This is a high grade-A answer because it deals with the basic points and demonstrates a number of interesting additional items, such as the differential effect on the Conservatives and the advantages for nationalist parties. It is a good example of what an able and well-prepared candidate can do.

(d) We have seen that it is mainly the Labour and Conservative parties which gain from FPTP. I shall look first at the results of this feature and then at how the political system is affected.

Since the Second World War, one party has always won the election outright. There was one exception in 1974 when Labour formed a minority government and won a general election majority a few months later. All this means that we elect a single party with a clear manifesto. We then know what the government's policies are and we can judge them accordingly. If we had coalition governments, which occur with PR, we would never be sure what the policies of the government would be. There is a decisive result and we do not have minority governments or unstable coalitions. FPTP brings us stable and certain government.

The political results of this are that the government is always able to control the House of Commons. Because there is a majority in parliament, the government is almost guaranteed to have its legislation passed. Some say this is a good thing as it makes for certainty. Others claim it is bad because it is difficult for parliament to control government. Lord Hailsham called the system an 'elective dictatorship'.

Parliament is also not representative in that small parties are not included. Many people want the Greens to be represented but they do not vote for them as this is seen as a wasted vote. So there is a Catch 22 situation. The Greens win no seats because of FPTP and few people vote for them because they win so few seats.

So we can see that the effects of FPTP are both good and bad. It depends whether you prefer stable government with a clear majority or whether you want parties properly represented with government being weaker.

e Another clear grade A for a well-planned answer. The student develops each point and uses a full range of political knowledge.

e **This is an excellent grade-A response by a candidate who has developed wide political knowledge throughout the course and writes clearly.**

Grade-C/D answer to question 2.2

(a) In each constituency the winner who takes the seat is the person who wins most votes. This is why it is called FPTP. For example, if candidate A wins 40% of the votes, candidate

B wins 35%, and candidate C wins 25%, candidate A is the winner even though he or she does not have more votes than the others put together.

e A grade-B response which is accurate and uses a sound example. The answer is not top grade because it omits to emphasise clearly enough the fact that the winner has no overall majority and that this occurs in many, though not all, constituencies. The student should have stated that each voter has only one vote.

(b) The elections to the Scottish and Welsh parliaments use a system like Germany's. It is called the AMS and is a mixed system where half the seats are gained FPTP and the rest are by a list system. Each voter has two votes, one for the constituency and one for a party. The votes for the party are added up and the seats are won in proportion to the votes. So if a party has 50% of the votes it gets half the seats. This helps the smaller parties which win no constituencies but get some seats from the lists. Some people voted one way with one vote and for another party with the other vote. The Greens even won some seats and the nationalists did quite well too. They did not do well in the general election. This system is fairer but a little complicated.

e A muddled account with a number of errors. The candidate has a basic idea of the system and merits a grade D as there are just enough facts here. It is predictable that knowledge of an alternative system may be required for an exam answer, so this part of the specification should be well learned.

(c) FPTP helps some parties more than others. It helps the large parties because they have support in some areas of the country and so win plenty of seats. They do not need to have overall majorities in all the seats. To illustrate this, Labour won the 1997 election by 179 seats with only 44% of the vote. This was because of the effects of FPTP. The Labour Party has plenty of support in the north and Midlands while the Conservatives do better in the south. The Liberal Democrats have support all over the country, but not enough to win many seats.

Small parties get a bad deal. They come second in many seats but cannot get enough votes in most constituencies to win the seat. In 1997, they won nearly 20% of the votes but only got 46 seats. The same goes for Plaid Cymru and the Scottish Nationalists. If there was a proportional system, these small parties would win more seats. Under FPTP the Greens win none at all.

This is an unsatisfactory state of affairs. Voters are not treated equally and parties are not properly represented in parliament.

e This is a much better answer than the previous ones and good enough to gain a borderline B/C grade. There are still omissions and errors — the nationalists actually gain from the system, while the Liberal Democrats have concentrated support in the southwest. But the candidate does make the basic points accurately and the powers of expression have been improved by the preparation.

(d) FPTP means that one party always wins an overall majority in parliament. So one party is always able to win outright and form a government. This is much better than having coalitions. Italy has had 50 governments since the war whereas British government is stable, the system is clear and we know where we are. Only once in modern times (in 1974) has one party failed to be able to form a government alone. We can see in Scotland and Wales what is the result of not using FPTP. So on balance we should keep the system as it is.

e This is a weak response to the part of the question which carries most marks. The candidate gets a C or D-grade mark for knowing the basic facts and understanding the main aspect of the system, but is under-prepared and rather muddled. The candidate should have been prepared to answer this question or something along similar lines. If the problem was insufficient time, the student should have used bullet points to cover the ground.

e **Overall, this is a patchy performance owing to lack of preparation.**

Question 2.3

Study the following data:

FPTP and AMS compared in Scotland

Party	Proportion of the seats won under FPTP in the 1997 general election	Proportion of the seats in the Scottish Parliament won under AMS in 1999
Labour	77.8 %	43.4 %
Liberal Democrat	13.9 %	13.2 %
Conservative	0	14.0 %
Scottish Nationalist	8.3 %	27.1 %
Green	0	0.8 %
Socialist	0	0.8 %
Other	0	0.8 %

Results of the 1997 general election, actual and AV+ (Jenkins proposal) compared

Party	Seats actually won in 1997	Estimate of seats likely to have been won under AV+
Labour	419	378
Conservative	165	160
Liberal Democrat	46	88
Scottish Nationalist and Plaid Cymru	10	14
Others (incl. N. Ireland)	19	19

Source: *Success in Politics*, Neil McNaughton, John Murray, 2001.

(a) (i) Briefly describe the operation of the additional member system (AMS). (6 marks)
(ii) Briefly describe the operation of the proposed alternative vote (AV+) system. (6 marks)

(b) (i) Why do the data indicate a difference in the performance of the parties under first-past-the-post (FPTP) compared with the additional member system? (10 marks)
(ii) Why do the data indicate a difference between the performance of the parties in the 1997 general election and as estimated under AV+? (10 marks)

(c) What evidence is there in the data to support the arguments for the introduction of proportional representation for general elections? (28 marks)

(d) What are the main arguments against the introduction of proportional representation for general elections? (30 marks)

Grade-A mark scheme for question 2.3 (65%+)

(a) The systems will be fully and accurately described. In the case of AMS, examples of how this operates in practical ways will be included. The full implications in terms of voting, seat allocation and selection of candidates will be explained.

(b) The reasons for the performance differences will be described, noting the proportional nature of parts of the system. Particularly strong answers will note that both systems favour third parties, but not necessarily very small parties. However, answers will note that Greens and others did gain some seats. The fact that the Liberal Democrats do well with AV+ will be noted (some especially strong candidates may note that Lord Jenkins, who proposed the system of AV+, is a Liberal Democrat).

(c) The evidence from the data revealing the stronger showing for small parties under PR will be extracted from both tables. There will be clear descriptions of how the party system is likely to change under these systems and explanations of why these may be favourable developments. This will mainly centre on the more representative nature of the House of Commons and the reduction in the control of the ruling majority party. The increased representation of small parties such as the Greens will be noted. Use will be made of examples from other political systems and from the experience of devolution in the UK.

(d) Arguments will centre on the likelihood that no party will win overall control under PR. The consequences of such results will be explored, to include an assessment of the possible negative results of coalition or minority government. Examples from other political systems will be used to illustrate the arguments. The possible negative effects of the stronger showing of small parties will be described. Any other arguments will be granted credit, provided they are properly justified.

Grade-A answer to question 2.3

(a) **(i)** The AMS is a mixed system. It is used in Scotland and Wales and also in Germany where a half or more of the seats are elected by FPTP. This means that the candidate with the largest vote is elected even if this is not a majority. There are also some seats (half in Germany, about a third in Scotland) which are elected by a top-up regional list system. This means voters vote for a party list as well and seats are awarded according to the proportion of these votes won. However, there is a bias built in whereby the parties which do badly in FPTP are given extra top-up seats. This makes the system more proportional.

(ii) The Jenkins Commission recommended the AV+ system. It is the same as the AMS with the following differences: the additional vote means that voters place candidates in order of preference; if a candidate gets 50% of first preferences, that candidate is elected; if nobody achieves a majority, the second preferences are added and so on until somebody has over half the votes. This system is used in Australia. The other seats are awarded proportionally, as with AMS.

e This is close to a perfect answer. The candidate was fully prepared for a predictable question, knows the facts and sticks to basic description. Everything is to the point and no time is wasted in this good example of how to answer short definitional questions.

(b) **(i)** The big difference between the results under AMS and FPTP is given in the table showing Scotland's results. We can see how Labour's proportion of seats fell dramatically under AMS from 77.8% to 43.4%. So Labour failed to gain an overall majority in Scotland, which it did easily in the general election. The Liberal Democrat performance is interestingly almost unchanged. But it was the Conservatives and the SNP who gained most. The Tories won no seats in the general election, but got 14% of the seats in the Scottish parliament. All these seats were gained in the regional list part of the system. The SNP got over three times as many seats under AMS in 1999. This transformed their representation in the Scottish parliament compared to Westminster. Finally, look at the small parties and an independent. No seats under FPTP of course, but each won a seat under AMS. So AMS gives a good chance to small groups.

(ii) It is interesting that AV+ makes little difference to most of the parties. What they gain under the list system, they lose under AV. The gainers are the Liberal Democrats who would pick up AV seats because they often come second and would pick up many second preference votes. Their seats were estimated to rise from 46 to 88. The others are little changed. Interestingly Labour would still have won an overall majority.

e Another excellent pair of answers which demonstrate how to deal with short stimulus–response questions. The candidate addresses the question and responds to all parts of the data thoroughly. AV+ could have been analysed a little more, although this might have cost too much time. Another good grade A.

(c) The results give us many arguments for introducing proportional representation for general elections as well as for the Scottish parliament. The main reason is that the smaller parties are given a fairer representation. We see how the Conservatives win a good number of seats under AMS but none under FPTP, which is a ridiculous state of affairs. The data also show how Labour's advantage is hugely exaggerated. This gives the government more power than it really deserves. AMS puts it right.

It is also true that small parties, such as the SNP and the Greens, do better, and it is important that minority groups like this get good representation. Under AMS they do. This is equally true of the Liberal Democrats whose seats nearly doubled under AV+ and who won a good number of seats in Scotland under AMS. This avoids votes being wasted and means that people can vote for their first choice rather than voting tactically. So we can say that the data prove that PR is a fairer system, gives better representation and avoids one party becoming too powerful.

e Another good example of strong technique for a good grade A. The student has stuck to the data as instructed, using them to illustrate the main points, which have been made clearly. A neat summary presses home the argument. Time was saved by not going beyond the data.

(d) Although there are many arguments in favour of the introduction of PR in general elections, there are also strong reasons against. The main one is that 'if it ain't broke, don't fix it'. FPTP produces strong, decisive government, which the British like. Single parties always win elections under FPTP so we don't have to deal with weaker coalition governments as is the case in Italy or France.

We should note too that FPTP is a simple system that everyone can understand. We place our vote and we know who wins. It also preserves the close link between an MP and a constituency, which is very important in the British system.

But perhaps the most important reason for having a system that almost guarantees one party wins is the system of mandate we have. Each party produces an election manifesto and, if elected, we can judge whether it has carried out its promises. If we had PR and smaller parties gained more seats, we would have coalitions. Under a coalition the voters do not know what they are getting. Tony Benn has said that this gives a government (coalition) that nobody has voted for.

The evidence from Scotland and Wales on PR is not good. They both have coalitions which are constantly arguing. For example, Labour and the Lib Dems could not agree over student fees in Scotland. This is what we might expect in Britain if we had a PR system.

So, if we wish to retain Britain's strong and decisive system of government with more predictable results, clear manifestos, good MP-constituency relations and a system which people can understand, we should certainly keep FPTP for general elections.

e A splendid A-grade answer awarded for a clearly planned mini-essay. The candidate sticks to the question — arguments *against* PR only — and resists the temptation to include arguments in favour of PR. Most of the points are mentioned with appropriate examples and a firm conclusion rounds up the points.

e **Overall, this is a high grade-A response that demonstrates the virtues of a good candidate in stimulus-response questions. The student is prepared for predictable questions, answers the questions precisely, uses the data effectively and has good structure for the longer answers, with firm conclusions. This is first-class technique.**

Parties and pressure groups

Question 3.1

Read the following passage:

Do pressure groups really maintain pluralism?

Does the existence of pressure groups really help to maintain a system where power is dispersed? Grant (1997) argues that declining party membership and the establishment of elements of a dominant party system in Britain has two important implications for pressure groups.

Firstly, it increases their importance as a mechanism for questioning and opposing government policy. Secondly, party factionalism gives them a new set of targets (dissident party groups) at which they can direct their activities.

Pressure groups seek to influence political decisions with varied degrees of success. However, there are relatively few decisions in which pressure groups are not involved in some way. Far more citizens are involved in pressure groups than political parties, whether through short-term local campaigns to, for example, stop a particular development, or a longer-term commitment to a trade union, a professional organisation or a cause group of some sort.

More of the general public are active in pressure groups than in political parties. Politicians have to listen to (and often act upon) the aims of pressure groups. Power, however, is still strongly held by the political parties due to their constitutional role in forming the executive. Dwindling party memberships probably result from people being more interested in particular issues and their livelihoods than in the broader coalition of interests represented in parties.

Source: 'How pressure groups influence parties', Deborah Outhwaite, *Politics Review*, Vol. 10, No. 2, November 2000.

(a) For what reasons does the extract suggest that more people are members of pressure groups than parties? (6 marks)

(b) Using information from the extract and your own knowledge, explain the main differences between pressure groups and political parties. (12 marks)

(c) What factors are likely to determine whether pressure groups are likely to be successful in achieving their aims? (22 marks)

Grade-A mark scheme for question 3.1

(a) All the relevant points should be included and well explained, particularly the suggestion that pressure groups have become more important than political parties. They influence virtually all policy areas. The extract suggests that people have become more focused on their own interests and livelihoods and on specific issues rather than the full range of policy. There is also an implication that people do not want to take on the levels of commitment which parties require.

(b) The main distinction the passage refers to is the fact that pressure groups concentrate on particular issues whereas parties have to deal with a wide range of public policy. It is also now true that pressure groups often have bigger memberships than political parties. Both these points should be included and other distinctions identified as well. These are: pressure groups do not normally put up candidates for election (except for some single-issue groups) and certainly do not seek governmental office; parties have to be politically responsible for their actions while pressure groups will not be held to account for their beliefs or actions; pressure groups often use direct action (which is sometimes illegal), while parties operate through more formal channels. Better responses will also include party organisation, and will point out that political parties are concerned with policy formulation and do not provide services for members.

(c) The size of a pressure group is important in determining the political pressure it can exert on government and access to finance. Its strategic position in society is also relevant. Environmental groups such as Friends of the Earth (FoE) or the Royal Society for the Protection of Birds (RSPB) are good examples. Wyn Grant's insider and outsider distinction should be used: groups such as the National Farmers' Union (NFU) or the Confederation of British Industry (CBI) are classic insiders which are constantly consulted and have direct access to those in political power; they also have leverage because government depends on their cooperation. Outsiders such as Greenpeace are able to influence government if they are able to mobilise public opinion. There are a number of other factors, most of which should be referred to, including finance, organisation, celebrity support, ideological empathy with the government and media support. Any other reasonable factors may be used, if justified by evidence.

■ ■ ■

Grade-A answer to question 3.1

(a) Pressure groups are mainly concerned with a single issue or a narrow range of issues whereas political parties have to deal with the complete range of policies. Many people are not interested in all political issues. Instead they are worried about what affects them directly or they have special interests such as the environment, animal rights or public transport. It is better for them to be active in pressure groups rather than parties. For this reason the passage suggests that more people are members of pressure groups than parties. There is also the time and commitment demanded by parties, something which many people prefer not to make. We are a pluralist society today so pressure groups reflect this. The passage suggests these points about parties and pressure groups.

e This is a grade-A example of the stimulus–response technique: the student has read the passage carefully and then deployed knowledge to explain the points raised in it. The candidate also noticed the title of the piece and goes a little beyond the text to discuss the relevant issue of pluralism.

(b) As I have discussed in section (a), the main difference between pressure groups and parties is the range of issues they deal with. Most cause groups such as FoE and the League against Cruel Sports deal with a single issue. Interest groups such as the CBI or Age Concern may be broader in their focus, but they are still only concerned with their members' interests. Political parties are different in two ways. First, they have to be concerned with all sections of the population. Second, they have to develop policies on all political issues. This is suggested by the passage, which also points out that parties are now only for activists who want to make a full political commitment. The large pressure groups have mass memberships who do not have a full-time commitment.

There are several other important differences between parties and pressure groups. The main one is that parties are hoping to form a government or to share in power in a coalition. This changes the way they behave. They have political leaders and have to fight elections in constituencies. Some pressure groups have put up candidates and the Green Party started as a pressure group. But the important difference concerns government. Parties have to balance their policies and one day may be made responsible for their actions. Pressure groups do not need to worry so much about other groups and counter-policies.

Pressure groups often use direct methods of campaigning such as mass demonstrations (note the Countryside Alliance's rallies in London) and illegal activities (Greenpeace destroying genetically modified (GM) crops). Parties cannot do this. They have to be responsible for their actions and certainly should not act illegally. They work mostly through democratic institutions.

There are several other more minor differences, too numerous to describe fully here. These are the formal organisation of parties, the way they choose leaders, the way they use the media and so on.

e Again, this is a high grade-A response. Although most candidates will not reach this standard of writing and will not have read so much, there are important lessons to be learned here. The first is to be properly prepared for the kind of question likely to arise within a topic. The second is to differentiate between the important points and the less important ones. The third is to use appropriate illustrations. The answer also exemplifies a good use of time where marginal points are mentioned at the end without any unnecessary expansion. This avoids the problem of running out of time later.

(c) There are some pressure groups which do better than others and I shall attempt to analyse why this is so by looking at specific groups. Some have been successful and some have failed. Before starting, it is essential to define success. I take it to mean that policy has been affected or changed in accordance with the wishes of the group concerned.

First, there is the issue of GM crops. Greenpeace and FoE have not stopped experiments but have succeeded in forcing the government to take precautions and limit the extent of the tests. They also stopped the sale of GM foods in most places. Greenpeace did this because it mounted successful publicity campaigns and also had the resources to mount publicity stunts like destroying crops. FoE is an insider group which consults with government. It has enough members to exert an influence and also provides information to government about the environment and so has won respect.

The two pressure groups for the aged — Help the Aged and Age Concern — have had great success in improving the deal for pensioners. This is mainly to do with their size. They have told government that there are millions of votes to be won or lost, so they need to address their problems. But size is not the only issue. Farmers, though a relatively small group, do well because they are organised and government knows they have a vital place in society. Money helps a great deal. The brewers campaigned for years for extended licensing hours and recently won the argument. The successful fuel lobby won its case by catching the public imagination and gaining press support.

Some campaigns win great public sympathy. The anti-smoking group, Action on Smoking and Health (ASH), for example, had the support and the organisation to influence the government's restrictions on tobacco advertising.

Some groups lose the ear of government, such as trade unions, and so they have less success. Small groups with little funding have great difficulty. Groups that are outsiders or do not have public sympathy or run against the beliefs of the government are likely to fail. The Campaign for Nuclear Disarmament (CND) never succeeded even though it had many members.

The question of why some groups do better than others is a difficult and complex one. Despite all the factors, luck and events often play a big part.

e This outstanding student gains another grade A with close to full marks. The particular strength of this answer is its exceptional use of examples and the way the whole essay is shaped around them. The candidate must have learned this response well and, when running short of time, packaged up several minor points in a concise ending. There are omissions, but the overall quality makes up for them. The candidate, who probably knows a good deal more than is revealed in this answer, resisted the temptation to carry on over the time allocated.

e **Many lessons can be learned from these answers, even by those who do not write so well and who do not have the breadth of knowledge. The use of limited time is especially impressive. Overall, this is a good grade-A response.**

Grade-B answer to question 3.1

(a) There is no doubt that pressure groups are steadily becoming more politically important than parties. The passage clearly suggests this. People do not want to make a full commitment to a political party and are more interested in the issues which affect them than those which affect the country as a whole. They therefore find it more useful to join pressure groups than parties. All this is included in the passage.

e This is a solid grade-A answer of which the main strength is the candidate's use of the required information using their own words. All points identified in the mark scheme are included for an ideal stimulus–response answer.

(b) The passage says that pressure groups deal with narrow issues, usually ones affecting the interests of their members. It states clearly that parties deal with a wide range of issues and also says that pressure groups are now more significant than parties.

The main distinction between a political party and a pressure group is that parties fight elections whereas pressure groups do not. Some pressure groups, such as the anti-gun Snowdrop Campaign and the Right to Life Campaign against abortion, do endorse candidates. Parties are hoping to become the government by winning elections whereas pressure groups are merely hoping to influence government.

Parties face the fact that they may become the government. This means that they must act within the law and have policies for all issues. They must also select their leaders carefully and accept the limitations of a democracy. Parties have members who donate money, while pressure groups have a more difficult task to raise money. Many pressure groups are small and narrow. They hope to gain some publicity and catch the spirit of public opinion. Parties are normally much larger and find it easier to gain publicity.

e This is a grade B because the candidate seems unprepared and, after a clear opening, strings out more marginal points at the end. There are not enough examples and some less important points are omitted. This is a predictable question and a good candidate should have prepared for it. The quality of the writing deteriorates as the student becomes less sure of the material.

(c) The most important factor in the success of pressure groups is whether they are insiders or outsiders. An insider is a group that is incorporated into the government in some way. Its members will be consulted regularly and may sit on government committees. They have close links with ministers and civil servants and can often give information to government. Some unions are insiders with Labour, and business groups are insiders with the Conservatives.

Outsiders, like the Animal Liberation Front (ALF), are not consulted and so have less success. These groups have to try to gain public support and so threaten the government because of the votes at stake. Groups which have a very large membership do not need to be insiders. They will have plenty of money and can gain a great deal of publicity for their cause.

Some groups share the ideology of the government and they will certainly enjoy success. So too will those pressure groups which enjoy widespread support among the public, perhaps by harnessing media campaigns and the backing of celebrities. They may also be well organised and so be able to make their case effectively.

Some large groups have the finance to mount public campaigns, advertise their cause and campaign among the public. Some may also sponsor MPs to put their case in parliament and may hire the services of professional lobby groups.

It is therefore clear that the important factors are: insider status, finance and size of membership. These are the reasons why some groups are more successful than others.

e This is a grade-B response which could have been a grade A had the candidate used some more examples. It is important to give examples of actual groups which have succeeded and groups which have failed with some assessment of reasons why this is so.

e **The grade B which is awarded reveals a candidate who showed ability but omitted too many points and didn't use enough examples to illustrate the answers.**

■ ■ ■

Question 3.2

Read the following passage:

Parties and pressure groups

The modern British political system is characterised by the fact that the importance of parties is in sharp decline, while the significance of the impact of pressure groups is steadily growing. The question is: 'Why is this happening?'

Parties are suffering from a number of problems that seem to be irreversible. Membership is falling rapidly and markedly, which deprives political parties of finance and, perhaps more importantly, of the activists who are so necessary for fighting elections. The loss of members and activists mean that it is more difficult to recruit members. Parties are also suffering the results of a general decline in respect for politicians. This is clearly demonstrated by falling election turnouts. At the same time, there is a general perception that governments cannot achieve as much as they claim they can.

In contrast, pressure groups are growing in number, in strength and in importance. This is a reflection of a much more pluralist society. With the wider range of interests that people have, increasing affluence and the fragmentation of the traditional class system, people find it inappropriate to identify closely with parties. Instead they see their interests and their causes better represented by pressure groups. It seems that pressure groups can achieve results while parties and governments cannot.

Original material

(a) Why does the passage suggest that pressure groups are now more important than parties? (12 marks)

(b) What is meant by the assertion that the British political system is now pluralist in nature? (20 marks)

(c) In what senses do pressure groups enhance democracy? (28 marks)

(d) Why are some pressure groups more successful than others? (30 marks)

Grade-A mark scheme for question 3.2 (65%+)

(a) The reasons for the growing importance of pressure groups stated in the passage should be identified and described. The loss of party members should be referred to, noting that activists are especially important, and that this is reflected in problems in obtaining finance. Low turnouts at elections and falling membership are partly the result of declining respect for politicians in general. The pluralist system must be identified, noting that it results in a multiplicity of interests which are better represented by pressure groups than by parties. Finally, the apparent greater efficacy of pressure groups should be noted.

(b) A full and well-illustrated response is required. The two main aspects of pluralism should be identified, namely the multiplicity of political beliefs and the fragmentation of interests. The best answers will refer to the decline in class cleavage and its replacement by pluralism. The increase in affluence means that people have more leisure pursuits. The growth in causes should also be identified with examples such as environmentalism, animal rights, countryside issues or similar. This results in fragmentation of political movements.

(c) Most of the ways in which pressure groups enhance democracy should be identified and appropriate examples used. There may be one or two omissions, but most of the main aspects must be included: acting as channels of communication with government; supplying information; educating and informing the public; protecting minorities; dissipating the power of the state and similar.

(d) Most, though not necessarily all, of the main factors will be described and exemplified. These are likely to include: size of membership (the Automobile Association (AA), Help the Aged); the ability to mobilise public support (Countryside Alliance); strong financial backing from producer groups (the tobacco companies); and insider status (NFU, CBI); sympathy with the aims of the government, such as health groups under New Labour; and the use of celebrities, such as AIDS campaigners. Any other cogent factors will be credited, provided they are well justified. There may be some omissions, but most major factors must be included.

Grade-B answer to question 3.2

(a) The passage says we are now a much more pluralist system. This means that people no longer identify with just two or three parties, but have many different interests. This means that people believe that they can achieve their goals by joining and working with pressure groups rather than with parties. Pressure groups have more members than parties, a clear sign that they are more important.

e Here is a concise, accurate answer, but the candidate has taken brevity too far and not searched the passage thoroughly enough. There is no reference to the decline of class cleavage, the loss of respect for politicians and of lower turnouts at elections. The response is on the borderline between a low B and a high C.

(b) Pluralism, as the passage says, means the decline of the traditional class system when everyone thought of themselves as either working, middle or upper class. They also tended to support either the Labour or Conservative parties. Pluralism means people tend to join pressure groups and are beginning to support a wider range of parties. We now have mostly consensus politics where there is little difference between the beliefs of the two main parties, so people have a range of different beliefs, for example over issues such as the environment, transport, or Europe and the single currency.

e This is a borderline A/B response in which the student shows an understanding of pluralism. The problem is that it could have been more developed and, in particular, might have noted how greater affluence means people have a wider range of issues in which they are interested. The candidate should also have noted that the decline of class cleavage means people have developed greater self-interest, hence movements such as the Countryside Alliance and the fuel lobby.

(c) Pressure groups are an important part of the modern democracy and the article tells us that parties are now much less important. We need parties and pressure groups for a number of reasons. I shall describe them and then assess the importance of pressure groups in a democracy.

The main importance is that pressure groups help to tell the government what people want. This is a two-way process because pressure groups help to educate the public in political issues, and simultaneously educate the government in the demands of the people.

Some pressure groups campaign for people's rights and without them sectors of the population would not be represented properly. As the article says, less and less people are now members of political parties while some groups, such as the RSPB, have mass membership. Pressure groups give an opportunity for people to take part in politics when they do not want to be involved in political parties.

Pressure groups often help government with decision-making. These are known as insider groups because they are consulted regularly, give important information and often appear on policy-making government committees and quangos. They are thus part of a representative democracy.

In conclusion, we can see how important pressure groups are. This is mainly because parties have fewer members and less influence. However, their main importance is in making sure that all groups in society are properly represented.

e This variable answer adds up to a borderline grade-B/C response. It is not very well expressed and there are a couple of major omissions. Only one example is used — the RSPB — when there were several opportunities to add illustrations. However, it has a good structure with a sound conclusion. Several important points are clearly understood and described, and the answer also does well in using information from the text provided. It would have been a solid grade B, had some more examples been used, and could have crept up to an A grade if two additional points had been raised.

(d) The main difference in pressure groups is whether they are insiders or outsiders. Insiders are those groups consulted by government and which may also have influence in parliament and on policy committees. Examples of insiders are FoE, the National Trust and the CBI. Outsiders, like trade unions and the ALF, often do not enjoy the ear of government and find success harder to achieve. Other outsider groups, the fuel lobby being a good recent example, manage to succeed in some of their aims.

Large pressure groups do well. Help the Aged is such a group, as is the RSPB, which has over 600,000 members. If a pressure group has a lot of members, the government can gain votes by supporting its cause. The same is true of money. Wealthy businessmen give donations to parties, with Labour receiving donations from Bernie Ecclestone, and Michael Ashcroft contributing to the Conservatives. Pressure groups can also sponsor MPs to represent them in parliament. Well-organised groups often do well. Recently, the Countryside Alliance succeeded in stopping the ban on fox-hunting and the NFU has secured much help for agriculture.

In conclusion, we can see that a number of factors contribute to success. But the most important reason is when the pressure group is associated with the government party. Unions do better under Labour (look at the minimum wage) and business groups do better under the Conservatives. It does not matter too much whether groups have money or many members; it really depends on how close they are to the government.

e Here is another answer of variable quality where important points are missing. However, this is a grade B because the candidate has used the examples which were lacking in section (c). This makes a good deal of difference and, had the student used a couple more examples, this response may have achieved a grade A.

e **Although the performance is rather patchy, the candidate achieves an overall grade B. Lack of examples and some important omissions undermine a solid level of knowledge and some well-structured answers.**

Question 3.3

(a) What are the main functions of pressure groups? (5 marks)

(b) Describe two different types of pressure group. (10 marks)

(c) Why are some pressure groups more successful than others? (15 marks)

(d) What arguments can be advanced to support the view that pressure groups may operate against the interests of democracy? (20 marks)

Grade-A mark scheme for question 3.3

(a) A description of pressure groups' main functions must be included with explanations. One or two minor functions may be omitted but no major ones. Examples are not required in this section. Answers will refer to such functions as channels of communication between government and the governed, protection of minority rights, mobilising public support for certain issues, opportunities for political participation, providing information for government. Best answers will refer to the need for an independent civil society as a protection against over-powerful government.

(b) Answers are likely to differentiate between outsiders and insiders or between interest (sectional) and issue (cause) groups. Examples must be used appropriately. In each case, the meaning of the term should be fully described, a clear distinction made and there will be some development of the descriptions.

(c) Refer to the mark scheme for question 3.1, part (c). Note that there are only 10 minutes for this answer compared to 20 minutes in question 3.1. The explanations will inevitably be shorter, there may be fewer factors mentioned and illustrations will be shorter.

(d) No credit is given for arguments suggesting that pressure groups enhance democracy as this is not asked. A good range of points will be included with appropriate illustrations. Answers are likely to include points such as the disproportionate influence of wealthy groups and that some pressure groups may not act in a responsible way. Examples of groups which exert undue influence should be used, with mention that the influence is not balanced by political accountability. Contrast should be made with the way political parties have to be responsible and operate through democratic channels. All reasonable arguments will be credited, if properly explained and justified with evidence.

Grade-C answer to question 3.3

(a) Some pressure groups try to represent the interests of a section of society. These are known as interest groups. They lobby government and try to influence policy for their members. Some are consulted regularly on policies. Others are interested in a cause or issue. They mainly try to gain public and media support for an issue and so hope that this will influence the government when they demonstrate (literally, sometimes) that there is a great deal of support for an issue.

e This is a solid and accurate response, but it is not comprehensive enough for more than a grade C. Only two or three pressure group functions are referred to. Even in the short time available a couple more should have been included.

(b) Pressure groups are either insiders or outsiders. An insider group is thought to be part of a corporatist society where groups are brought into the government. Insiders have knowledge and information government wants and so they are consulted. Sometimes they sit on committees, give evidence to committees of MPs in parliament and may sponsor MPs. Examples are the NFU and the CBI. Unions were insiders under Old Labour, but not very much today. Outsiders are the opposite. Either government does not wish to consult them or they actually want to stay away from government so they are free to do as they wish. They tend to concentrate on mass campaigns and direct action to bring public attention to an issue. Examples are the Greenpeace environmental group and the fuel lobby's blockade over petrol prices.

e This is a grade-A answer with good examples and clear explanations. The student avoided the temptation (though it would have been permitted) to use the same classification as in part (a). However, marks for writing quality are not high, and a few content marks have been forfeited due to undeveloped explanations.

(c) Insider pressure groups are usually more successful because they have the ear of government and are important to them. The farm lobby, for example, gains many subsidies and grants from government because government thinks agriculture is important to the country. This is also true about trade unions and the Labour Party (though not Conservatives). Outsiders do not gain such advantages so that Greenpeace, for example, has failed to stop production of GM foods because it behaves in illegal ways.

Some groups have a great deal of money. Big producer groups like tobacco firms, newspapers and the drinks industry gain a great deal of influence. Sometimes they finance political parties and gain influence in that way. Bernie Ecclestone allegedly paid £1 million to New Labour to stop a ban on tobacco sponsorship (although Labour was asked to give this money back).

Finally, there are some groups which gain a great deal of public popularity. I will identify two of these. The first is the Countryside Alliance which has held big demonstrations in London and is hoping to stop the ban on fox-hunting. The other is the fuel protesters who gained such huge support among motorists that they forced Gordon Brown to reduce the tax on petrol.

So the three main factors for success are insider status, finance and having a great deal of public support.

e This is a borderline between B and C because the response is limited in the range of points and spends too much time on explanations of the three points that are included. The candidate loses marks for content but does gain marks for analysis, despite weak powers of expression. With more content and a little less description, this answer would have been on the A/B borderline.

(d) Pressure groups are a vital part of a modern democracy. I shall look at why they are important and why they may not be in the interests of democracy and then attempt to determine which argument is stronger.

Pressure groups give people the chance to participate in politics and make their views known to the government. Parties are less effective in doing this and membership is falling. Pressure groups tell government about opinions among the public and sometimes give government important information. Britain is a pluralist system and it is vital that we have free and active pressure groups.

On the other hand, pressure groups may damage democracy. Sometimes they pervert politics by giving large amounts of money to parties and candidates and so influence policies in this undemocratic way. The slogan that 'money talks' is true in politics. Big business and big trade unions can use their funds in this way, but having money does not make a pressure group representative of people's opinions.

Some pressure groups hold the government to ransom and may act illegally. Greenpeace threatens GM crop tests and the ALF tries to destroy laboratories where there are animal experiments. The anti-hunt lobby tries to disrupt fox-hunting. They should use legal political methods as the Countryside Alliance does. Other groups gain disproportionate influence because they gain the interest of the media or because a government is elected which is sympathetic to them.

On balance, pressure groups are good for democracy despite the reasons I have explained which may damage democracy. The answer is that there are some pressure groups that are good for democracy and others which act against the interests of democracy.

e The question specifically asks for only one side of the argument and not two. The student has committed a serious error in answering a different question from the one asked. Credit goes to the sections of the answer that address the question, but there are no marks for the overall assessment attempted. This limits content and analysis marks. This only merits a grade D. More marks would have been available if the candidate had addressed the question properly.

e **Overall, this is a grade-C answer for a candidate who, but for sloppy exam technique, could have earned a high grade B or a borderline A.**

Topic 4

Parliament and parliamentary reform

Question 4.1

Read the following extract:

We have proposed a largely appointed chamber with a relatively small elected element. Our system of democracy and indeed our terms of reference require that the House of Commons remains the pre-eminent house. The Commons are directly elected and, while a government has the support of the House of Commons, it can stay in office. If it loses that support, it goes.

Many of those who have been sympathetic to much of the analysis in our report part company with us at this point. They argue that by recommending a largely appointed house, the Royal Commission has undermined its own arguments and that the reformed House of Lords should have at least a majority of elected members if it is to have the authority and legitimacy to act as a real restraint on the executive.

But it would inevitably be the case that a second chamber that sought to challenge the House of Commons on the basis of its electoral mandate would lose. It would be undemocratic to suggest anything else. In any event, none of the political parties would support it and the House of Commons wouldn't vote for it. So the reformed second chamber will have to rely on other sources of authority anyway. We believe these should include:

- the extent to which the members of the chamber are broadly representative of the society they seek to serve
- the breadth of experience and range of experience they possess
- individual personal distinction
- the quality of the arguments they bring to bear
- the ability to exercise an unfettered judgement, free from partisan political control

Source: 'Lords reform', Lord Wakeham, *Politics Review*, Vol. 10, No. 2, November 2000.

(a) What is Lord Wakeham's view of the appropriate relationship between the House of Lords and the House of Commons? (5 marks)

(b) What qualities does the passage suggest that appointed members of the House of Lords should possess? (10 marks)

(c) What arguments can be made in favour of proposing a wholly elected House of Lords? (15 marks)

(d) What arguments can be suggested for significantly enhancing the powers of the House of Lords? (20 marks)

Grade-A mark scheme for question 4.1 (65%+)

(a) This should be an interpretation of Lord Wakeham's views, referring to his recognition that the Commons is the senior house, that the electoral mandate of the Commons is superior and that the Commons is responsible for its actions while the Lords is not. Wakeham refers to legitimacy giving the Commons the authority to challenge government that the Lords does not possess.

(b) Qualities of appointed lords should be identified and explained with some extension of the material in the passage. Each of the bullet points should be developed and examples of specific peers or types of peer used.

(c) This requires a well-developed set of arguments but not the counter-arguments. It is likely that the following points will be included: the need for accountability; the requirements of democracy; the possibility that the House of Lords will become more representative (though this may be expressed as problematic); the possibility that a Lords with elective authority would become an effective counterbalance to the power of the Commons and the government. The use of different election systems and different terms of office should be explored. Any other reasonable arguments will receive credit, if well argued.

(d) Only arguments in favour of strengthening the House of Lords are needed. There will be a full discussion of the problems associated with the power of the Commons majority and therefore government. There will be a full set of arguments for strengthening the existing functions of the Lords in European matters, non-partisan legislation, scrutiny, plus delaying and amending powers. Justifications for such strengthening will need to be well supported. The idea of checks and balances may be introduced, as may suggestions concerning regional affairs or rights issues.

■ ■ ■

Grade-B answer to question 4.1

(a) Lord Wakeham suggests that the House of Lords is not elected and so it can never have the same authority as the House of Commons. He wants the Commons to be the senior house. The House of Commons can remove a government from office whereas the Lords cannot do this as it has insufficient authority, even if it was partly elected.

> **e** This is a grade-B answer because, although the argument is well identified, the student has omitted important aspects concerning legitimacy and has not addressed the third paragraph of the passage. In stimulus–response questions it is important to respond to all relevant parts of the material.

(b) The qualities that appointed members of the Lords need are that they should be representative of society, have an area of expertise and good personal qualities and be able to argue points well. The passage also says they should be independent and not connected to any political party.

> **e** A grade C is awarded for picking out the correct points. However, candidates should expand on what is in the material and deploy some appropriate examples.

(c) Lord Wakeham suggests we should have a House of Lords which is partly appointed and partly elected. Many people argue that he should have followed the Liberal Democrat suggestions and recommended a fully elected House of Lords. There are several arguments for this.

Firstly, it would have more elective authority and so would be more respected. At the moment it is appointed and it is felt that it is just another quango appointed by the government. If it is to be part of the legislature, it has to be elected. This is the only democratic solution.

Secondly, it would be more representative because a wider variety of people would be elected. Now it is very narrow socially, being mostly elderly men. The House of Lords would also become accountable to the people for what it does. At the moment it can stop legislation — such as Clause 28 or the fox-hunting bill — yet is not accountable for what it is doing.

However, the most important factor is that the House of Commons is controlled by the government and has become an elective dictatorship. We need an elected second chamber to balance the power of the government. Of course, it would have to be elected in a different way and perhaps at different times. It could then have stronger amending powers and perhaps could stop extreme legislation. We need a stronger safeguard for our rights, and there are important moral and constitutional matters that an elected second chamber could decide.

e This is a strong, grade-A response. Each point is described reasonably fully within the limited time. One or two arguments have been omitted, but the main points are made.

(d) The first thing to say is that if the House of Lords is to be given more power, it would have to be elected. It would need more authority to have more power because power and authority should match. To have more authority, it would have to be made accountable. Now we can examine the main arguments for giving it more power.

The House of Commons is too weak and is becoming weaker. It is completely dominated by the executive branch and Lord Hailsham has described it as an 'elective dictatorship'. The reason is that the party whips dominate and there is now prime ministerial government. If we had an elected second chamber, it might be independent of party control and so balance the power of the government. This would be rather like the US system where Congress's majority is sometimes different from the president's party. They call this system 'checks and balances'. The Commons does not make government accountable enough and the House of Lords could take over this role.

The House of Lords plays a powerful role in checking European legislation. This could be strengthened as Europe grows more important. They could perhaps be given greater facilities for this role and might also be in greater control of issues which are constitutional or which deal with people's rights. They could have the power to amend legislation or in some cases to send it back for further consideration.

For these reasons we can see that the Lords could be made stronger and could play a useful role in controlling the power of government. It might also help to protect our rights both in the UK and from European legislation. Of course, this is provided it is an elected House.

e This solid answer has some well-made points and gets high marks for the quality of writing and analysis. However, there is less of a time constraint here and a number of additional points could have been made. Consequently, some content marks are missed. This reflects a candidate who needed to revise more thoroughly. This answer gets a borderline A/B grade.

e **A high grade B is awarded overall. Better content in part (d) or a stronger part (b) would have taken the candidate up to a grade A.**

Question 4.2

(a) Explain the functions of the House of Commons. (20 marks)

(b) How effectively does the House of Commons perform these functions? (20 marks)

Grade-A mark scheme for question 4.2 (65%+)

(a) All key Commons' functions will be included and explained. One or two less important functions may be omitted but all major ones must be included. Grade A will only be awarded to responses that discuss the role of legitimation — the formal process of granting democratic consent — and differentiate it from the idea of law-making.

(b) Answers will discuss the key functions and give a balanced assessment of how well the Commons performs them. Candidates will concentrate on making government accountable, redressing grievances, representing sections of the community, checking legislation and public finance, and amending legislation. Best answers will also discuss the Commons' role in maintaining the legitimacy of government.

Grade-B answer to question 4.2

(a) The House of Commons has a number of important functions and above all is the legislature whose main job is to make law. Some laws are proposed by private members but most are developed by the government. The Commons also considers amendments to laws and this is done by standing committees where groups of MPs discuss proposals to amend bills and may hear witnesses or ministers on the subject.

The second role is to question government and ministers and make them accountable. This is done through parliamentary questions, including prime minister's question time every Wednesday. However, the main role is played by select committees, which can question civil servants and ministers and others when investigating the work of government departments.

Thirdly, MPs can take up matters for their constituents and their constituency. For example, if there is to be a major development which might affect a quiet country district or if a major factory is to close down, the MP in the area might raise the matter in parliament. This is known as the redress of grievances and is the oldest function of parliament. MPs raise issues in the House and this gains publicity. They can do this at question time or in early day motions or under the Ten Minute Rule.

These are the main functions, although it can also be said that the House of Commons is a place where our elected representatives can discuss important issues.

e Although three or four functions are quite well described, a few are omitted (notably legitimation and its role in controlling finance). With a predictable question like this, it is important to be well prepared and learn a full range of functions. There is no overview of the House's role. This is a grade-C response, but a high one due to the quality of the writing and clear construction.

(b) The House of Commons' role as a legislator is weak. MPs do not have the time or the knowledge to look at legislation thoroughly and, more importantly, they are heavily whipped and rarely vote against their party leaders. This means that they are not looking thoroughly at new laws. They have the chance to amend bills in committee but again the whips have control.

The Commons also calls government to account. It does this quite well, especially in the select committees where ministers are subject to hard questioning. The MPs take their role in select committees very seriously. The foreign secretary, Robin Cooke, has been given a hard time as were agriculture ministers over foot and mouth. At question time, MPs do raise many questions, but it has descended into a shouting match.

Many MPs do a good job in looking after their constituents. They conduct local surgeries and ask questions in parliament. Because they have little power over policy, MPs are keen to help where they can — and that is in their own constituencies.

The House of Commons' members are not fully representative of the general population, so their role as a representative body is weakened. There are more women recently, but ethnic minorities are under-represented.

Overall, I would suggest that the Commons performs some of its functions effectively but that others are done badly, mainly because of excessive control by the whips and party leaders.

e This is a high grade-B response with well-argued points and a solid overall assessment. However, legitimation is again missing and the discussion on legislative functions is relatively uncritical. There is also nothing on financial matters. However, the candidate does well on most of the major issues.

e The candidate's exam technique and expression of ideas is good enough for a grade B. The problems are mainly due to lack of general political knowledge. Thorough reading on all the main institutions pays dividends in the exam.

Question 4.3

Read the following passage:

Britain's constitution is what governments can get away with. Although parliament is nominally supreme, it is being relegated to an unimportant backwater. Able to do anything except change a man to a woman (although these days authorising the operation to do that), parliament, in theory, controls the executive, but parties have taken its powers and made it just a noisy rubber stamp. MPs find solace in activity as unpaid party campaigners, overpaid social workers or amateur citizens' advice bureaux — all consolations for impotence.

This is not a truth MPs can tell their constituents, so they give the impression of leaving on Monday morning to do a spot of governing the country before returning to deal with their constituents' problems or they cite Bagehot's claim that MPs 'audit the executive'. In fact, ministers only fear being removed from office and, indeed, Bagehot (1826–77) wrote in a brief period when MPs could do that. Since then mass parties have made elections a plebiscite [referendum] between two (now two-and-a-half) parties. Only the electorate kicks ministers out and so the executive controls the legislature through the party majority.

Source: 'Backbencher's lament', Austin Mitchell, *Politics Review*, Vol. 10, No. 3, February 2001.

(a) What does the passage tell us about the relationship between the executive and parliament? (6 marks)

(b) Using the passage and your own knowledge, what are the main functions of MPs? (12 marks)

(c) How effective is parliament in making government accountable? (22 marks)

Grade-A mark scheme for question 4.3 (65%+)

(a) Only information from the extract will be given credit. It should be made clear that Austin Mitchell is suggesting parliament is merely a rubber stamp, and that while (in Bagehot's day) it once had control over government, this is no longer true. The idea that an election campaign is fought out in parliament should be identified as part of the relationship. It is essential that answers refer to the final statement that the executive controls the legislature through the party majority.

(b) The roles mentioned in the passage should all be identified, i.e. as social workers, citizens' advice bureaux and party campaigners. It should also be noted that Mitchell describes them as 'rubber stamps'. A range of other functions should be identified, including the nature of constituency work, committee functions both in and out of parliament, and involvement with pressure and interest groups. The possibility that MPs may effectively call ministers to account should be included. Any other functions may be credited, if effectively justified.

(c) A complete assessment should balance the arguments and give a clear evaluation of parliament's role. Such negative issues as control by the parties and the whips, a lack of research facilities and expertise, secrecy in government, effects of collective responsibility, lack of time and so on will be included. On the positive side, reference is likely to be made to the work of select committees, the questioning of ministers, improvements in facilities for MPs and the general fact that government must still report to parliament. There should also be discussion of the House of Lords and a mention that, in recent years, the Lords has proved an effective opposition. Any other aspects will be credited if accurately described and justified. Some illustrations, preferably from recent political life, should be included.

■ ■ ■

Grade-A answer to question 4.3

(a) The general idea in the passage suggests that parliament is really just a rubber stamp with Austin Mitchell saying that while MPs pretend they are part of the governing process, they are really politically impotent. He points out that things were different in Bagehot's day when parliament could audit the government. Now, though, he says parliament is completely controlled by the parties and their whips. He says that parliament has been reduced to the role of a general election campaign between the parties.

e This concise answer does all that is required for a grade A. The student has identified all the points, written them up clearly and the mention of Bagehot gives a perspective on the relationship.

(b) The passage is scathing about the role of MPs and says they are glorified social workers who pretend to their constituents that they are being effective when, in fact, they do very little. Mitchell says they are unpaid party workers who are really carrying out a 4-year election campaign which is directed by the party leaders.

But MPs do a great deal more than Mitchell is suggesting. They often sit on select committees where they can question ministers and get information out of them. This is very important in a democracy. They also do work on standing committees which amend legislation and sit on party policy committees. Many MPs are also working on behalf of pressure groups that are allowed to pay them a small retainer to represent them in parliament.

MPs raise matters of importance at times like adjournment debates and under the Ten Minute Rule. A few lucky MPs win a place in the ballot to introduce private members' bills and hope to get legislation through parliament. Even though this rarely succeeds, it does publicise the issue such as fox-hunting or reform of the House of Lords.

Perhaps the most important role of MPs is to represent their constituencies. When a constituent has a problem, an MP can raise the issue at question time or can lobby ministers directly. This is why Austin Mitchell calls them 'social workers'.

e This is an another grade-A answer in which the candidate uses material from the passage and extensive personal knowledge, and deploys examples successfully.

(c) It is important in a democracy that the government is made accountable, and parliament is the main way in which this is achieved. It is therefore a vital question as to how effectively it does this.

In some ways parliament is very effective. The House of Lords has checked the power of government recently on such issues as the repeal of Clause 28, privatisation of air traffic control and fox-hunting. Because the Lords is more independent, it is not so controlled by the whips, and the government must listen to it despite the limited powers of amendment and delay.

Strangely, the Commons appears weaker even though it is elected and has more authority in theory. It does not do a very good job in controlling government for a number of reasons. The party whips exercise a great deal of control over MPs who do not like to challenge their own government. This is partly because of party loyalty and partly because of the power of patronage. It is also true that MPs are really just amateurs. They have little detailed knowledge of most issues and have few research staff. A minister has a huge civil service machine while MPs have very little help. It is therefore difficult for MPs to challenge ministers.

The select committees are quite strong, but again the MPs on them often have limited knowledge and only a few researchers. Ministers and civil servants are also skilled in avoiding answering questions properly. At question time the same problems can exist.

Even so, MPs produce thousands of questions every year and they have to be answered. Ministers also know that they can be defeated, so they have to listen to MPs. Policies have to be approved by parliament and this is a discipline on government. We have seen MPs finding out valid information about issues such as Sierra Leone and the Keith Vaz issue.

The general picture is therefore mixed with some strengths and some weaknesses. Overall, however, Austin Mitchell is right in saying that parliament is dominated by government. MPs need to have more information and be more professional if they are to control government effectively. The House of Lords simply needs more power.

e This is a comprehensive answer and well worth a grade A. The evidence is balanced and the candidate arrives at a firm assessment which refers to the Lords and the Commons separately. This is a good example of how to tackle a mini-essay because it is both strong on discussion and focused. The candidate shows good technique in referring back to the text for additional evidence.

e **This candidate was well prepared and showed excellent techniques in using the stimulus effectively and in structuring answers. This strong A-grade response shows precision and sticks closely to the demands of the questions.**

The prime minister and cabinet

Question 5.1

(a) Distinguish between individual ministerial responsibility and collective ministerial responsibility. (20 marks)

(b) To what extent has individual ministerial responsibility become a myth? (20 marks)

Grade-A mark scheme for question 5.1 (65%+)

(a) Each of the principles of ministerial responsibility should be described with examples and illustrations to underpin the explanations. The different interpretations of the doctrines should be described as well as the current position with each.

(b) Answers will explore the development and erosion of the doctrine of individual ministerial responsibility with copious use of appropriate examples. Responses should be critical, while balancing the arguments that ministerial responsibility no longer exists with arguments that elements of it still survive.

■ ■ ■

Grade-A answer to question 5.1

(a) In a modern democracy, ministers have to be made responsible for their decisions. They are elected and must therefore be made publicly responsible. There are two ways this is done in Britain. One is that each minister is individually responsible for every decision made within his or her department. It does not matter whether they were personally involved; they are still responsible. This protects civil servants who may have made the error because they are not elected and not politically responsible. Being responsible means that ministers must account for their actions and decisions in parliament or in select committees. In extreme circumstances they may be asked to resign. I shall discuss in part (b) whether the principle is still valid and I shall give examples. However, I would point out that Lord Carrington resigned under this issue in 1982 because of mistakes made before the Falklands War.

When government makes a decision collectively it becomes collectively responsible, which means that everybody in the government is accountable together. This in turn means that the government could be removed from office by a vote of no confidence in the House of Commons. However, it is more important that ministers can all support the decisions which the government makes. They must all 'sing from the same hymn sheet'. If a minister disagrees in public, he must resign or will be sacked. Peter Kilfoyle resigned in 1999 because he disagreed with government economic policy. Michael

Heseltine resigned from Margaret Thatcher's government in the 1980s over the Westland dispute, when he disagreed with cabinet colleagues.

e This is an excellent response, attracting a grade A, because the candidate has produced clear descriptions of individual and collective responsibility and has distinguished between the two. Appropriate examples reinforce different aspects of each doctrine in a well-rehearsed response. The temptation to answer parts of section (b) in the first part have been avoided.

(b) The idea of individual ministerial responsibility is now almost dead in the water. There have been countless ministers in the 1990s who have been severely criticised but have remained in office. These include Michael Howard, who lost court cases over prison issues, and William Waldegrave and other ministers, who were criticised in the Scott Report in the 'Arms to Iraq' affair. More recently, Lord Falconer did not resign over the Dome disaster. The true picture now is that ministers only resign under two circumstances. One is when it is a very serious error they made themselves. The other is if the prime minister decides they should go, and this occurred when Tony Blair decided he had had enough of Peter Mandelson.

So ministerial responsibility is not a myth, in that ministers are still questioned and criticised and may resign if the prime minister wants them to. However, ministers are often very reluctant to resign even if an error they have made is quite serious.

e Once again, a high grade A is awarded for good examples, clear descriptions, the critical yet balanced arguments and a relevant conclusion. Many students will not share this degree of knowledge but can learn from the organised approach and realise the value of memorising good examples.

e **These are predictable questions and sensible students will prepare for them. The key point is to be as up to date as possible and to use contemporary examples. The definitions of the basic doctrines should be learned in the way this candidate has done.**

Question 5.2

(a) What are the main functions of the prime minister? (5 marks)

(b) What are the main constraints on prime ministerial power? (10 marks)

(c) To what extent is the prime minister able to control the cabinet? (15 marks)

(d) What arguments can be advanced to suggest that the prime minister is now effectively a president? (20 marks)

Grade-A mark scheme for question 5.2 (65%+)

(a) The main formal and informal prime ministerial functions have to be identified with a reasonable amount of development in the time available. One or two of the less important functions may be omitted.

(b) There should be a description of the concept of *primus inter pares* and an explanation of the prime minister's relationship to the cabinet. There should be examples of constraints on power such as: the size of the parliamentary majority; personal popularity; the state of the governing party; and external events. Each constraint will be fully explained and illustrated with examples.

(c) There will be a description of the prime minister's chairmanship of the cabinet and reference to the control of patronage, the cabinet agenda and minutes. Grade-A answers must go beyond these basic points and deal with the prime minister's use of inner cabinets, the manipulation of cabinet committees, bilateral arrangements with ministers, use of the Cabinet Office and senior officials, control of presentation of policy, briefings, spin doctors and so on. All reasonable pieces of evidence will be credited but they must be underpinned by real-world illustrations.

(d) The idea that the prime minister has presidential powers and adopts a presidential style should be explained. The belief that the prime minister's role and powers have increased and the nature of these changes will be explained. Reference will be made to examples, such as the growing importance of the media in relation to the prime minister, the declining role of the cabinet, the growth of the advice available from the Cabinet Office and private advisers and the growing importance of foreign affairs. Such features should be directly compared with the position of a president, and the extent to which the changes now constitute a British presidency will be assessed. Counter-arguments need not be included. Reference to leading authorities such as Hennessy or Foley will receive credit, as will appropriate illustrations from recent premierships going back to Margaret Thatcher's.

■ ■ ■

Grade-C answer to question 5.2

(a) The prime minister has the power to appoint and dismiss all ministers. He or she decides who will be in the cabinet and cabinet committees and also appoints peers, bishops and judges and gives out honours. As chair of the cabinet, the prime minister controls the meetings (see below) and is the main policy-maker with power over foreign treaties. These are the main powers of the prime minister.

> **e** This is a grade-B answer which clearly identifies the basic prime ministerial functions, but which omits too many functions to be a grade A. The prime minister's party leadership, leadership in parliament and roles as chief government spokesperson should have been mentioned too.

(b) The prime minister depends on personal popularity. If he/she loses the support of the people, then he/she will find it difficult to exercise power and influence. The prime minister may also be outvoted in the cabinet. He cannot simply bulldoze everything through. If the prime minister loses his/her majority in the House of Commons he/she cannot really continue in office for very long. He/she may also lose the support of the party and cabinet colleagues. Finally, I would emphasise that the prime minister is not completely free to choose anybody for the cabinet or to be a minister. He/she may have to choose political enemies or people who have support in the party. This is a major constraint. However, it has to be emphasised that the powers of the prime minister far outweigh the constraints. I shall explore this point in section (d) below.

e This is another grade-B answer that includes the main points and expands on them reasonably well. The reason that this is not an A grade is that there are no illustrations. Examples of constraints from the experiences of Margaret Thatcher, John Major and Tony Blair would have completed a response which is otherwise sound.

(c) As chair of the cabinet, prime ministers control its meetings, decide everything that is discussed, remove anything they do not like from the agenda and also decide who will be in the cabinet and who is dismissed for causing trouble. Margaret Thatcher got rid of most of her enemies when they tried to defy her, and Harold Macmillan once sacked a third of his cabinet in what was called the 'night of the long knives'. Harold Wilson used to decide what was discussed and managed to side-step difficult issues.

Above all, the prime minister is party leader and so has control over policy. The cabinet cannot really defy a prime minister if the whole party has approved a policy. This is because the prime minister is still chief policy-maker. Other ministers run the department, but they have little say on overall policy. In theory, the Cabinet Office serves the cabinet as a whole but now it is believed that it serves the prime minister instead. In this and the other ways I have described, the prime minister exercises a great deal of control over the cabinet.

e This is a classic C-grade response. It has a number of points which are sound and well made. There is some attempt to go beyond the basics, but development of the points is limited. There are a few illustrations, unlike section (b), but they are a little dated. Examples using Tony Blair and John Major would be better. The writing is solid but of variable quality. The candidate needed to have prepared more up-to-date examples on recent developments under Blair: shorter cabinet meetings, private advisers and so on.

(d) It is often said that the prime minister today is more like a president than a head of government in having taken on more functions and developed a presidential style. I shall examine these beliefs in turn.

Firstly, the prime minister now has a huge number of advisers in the prime minister's policy unit, the Cabinet Office and with people such as Alastair Campbell. All this is beginning to resemble the White House machine which backs the US president.

Secondly, the press and media concentrate more on the prime minister, who represents the whole government. Prime minister's question time is a major event each week and is heavily reported. The prime minister is the mouthpiece of the government just as the president speaks for the American government.

Thirdly, the prime minister has taken over all the powers of the monarch as head of state, so that he/she is effectively as much head of state as the US president is. He/she has power to appoint all ministers and peers and to give out honours. He/she is also commander-in-chief of the armed forces and negotiates foreign treaties. A president carries out all these functions so there is a great similarity.

The general picture is therefore that the prime minister has become very much like a president because his/her powers have increased and he/she has adopted a more presidential style.

e This is a high grade-C response that raises several good points and explains them quite well. Once again there is a lack of examples and up-to-date information to underpin the points. The quality of the writing is satisfactory but unsophisticated. There is a weak attempt at assessment at the end, but this is not a balanced conclusion. There should be some reservations about the conclusions. Some important points have been raised, but there are also a few omissions.

e **Overall, this is a grade-C set of answers of which the main failing is that the candidate has not used up-to-date information and examples, and has omitted a number of points. A good set of notes on recent developments, especially since 1997, which could have been used as examples, would have been an asset. The issue of prime ministerial power has become more interesting since Tony Blair took over and there should have been more real-world examples.**

Question 5.3

Read the following passage:

There will be no returning to the traditional roles of the prime minister and cabinet which existed before the 1980s. That now seems certain. What is more difficult to predict is the extent to which current trends will be maintained and extended. All we can do is to summarise current developments and speculate that they will guide our thoughts in the immediate future. They are as follows:

- The prime minister and his/her cabinet play an increasing role in managing a more complex, pluralist political process. They are more facilitators than initiators. As individuals they must comprehend and control a complicated web of relationships in achieving desirable policy outcomes.

- The dissemination and manipulation of information is of growing importance to government. The media are increasingly influential, intrusive and informed. It is likely that a growing proportion of the time of the prime minister, ministers and their advisers will be spent in dealing with the presentation of policy.
- For similar reasons to those described in the previous point, the image of the prime minister and ministerial colleagues is of paramount importance. It may indeed become the case that this broad image proves more decisive than the actual content of policies themselves.
- Prime ministers have always had a number or roles to play. One of these roles, however, has assumed even greater importance. This concerns leadership of their own party.

Source: *The Prime Minister and Cabinet Government*, Neil McNaughton, Hodder and Stoughton, 1999.

(a) The passage states that prime ministers have always had a number of roles to play. What are these roles? (6 marks)

(b) How does the passage suggest that the roles of prime minister and cabinet are currently changing? (12 marks)

(c) From information in the passage and your own knowledge, to what extent do you believe that the British prime minister has effectively become a president? (22 marks)

Grade-A mark scheme for question 5.3 (65%+)

(a) See the mark scheme for question 5.2 (a). The points should be slightly better developed and possibly one or two more points may be included.

(b) Identifying the points is straightforward and includes all the bullet points in the second half of the passage. Expand on the points and illustrate with real-world examples. It is important in stimulus–response questions to use information from the stimulus and then to expand on it.

(c) See the mark scheme for question 5.2 (d). There is more time available in this example, so the analysis is likely to be more extensive and possibly one or two more minor points might be included.

■ ■ ■

Grade-A answer to question 5.3

(a) Prime ministers have both formalised constitutional roles which are unlikely to vary, and less formal political roles which are likely to change depending on who is prime minister and on the circumstances. The constitutional roles include patronage (appointment and dismissal of ministers, peers, judges etc.), chairing cabinet meetings, commanding the armed forces and dealing with national security. The prime minister also takes charge of important foreign policies and has to negotiate treaties with foreign powers and the EU.

The prime minister has informal political roles as well. The main one is the policy-making that is shared with the cabinet, ministers and the rest of the party. He also speaks for the whole government. This role is played in parliament and to the media. Finally, when it comes to parliament, it is the role of the prime minister to organise the party there. He has to lead and speaks for them.

e In a very solid A-grade response, most of the key functions are included and are explained with as much development as time allows.

(b) The passage suggests that the whole business of government is now more complicated. It is no longer clear where and how policies are being made. The phrase 'more facilitators than initiators' means that they do not make policy but simply make sure it can be carried out successfully.

Secondly, the passage says that the prime minister and cabinet are now more concerned with the presentation of policy. Managing the media has become important and we see this with the growing use of private advisers and spin doctors.

Thirdly, there is the question of image. The government is very concerned with being seen to be in control and decisive and united. This inspires confidence with the public and the media. They seem to be constantly fighting an election campaign, so they are worried about presentation and image.

Finally, the passage says that the prime minister's role of party leader has become much more important. I think this means that it is important to keep the party together and avoid the splits that damaged both Margaret Thatcher and John Major. Tony Blair has learned the lesson and tried to control New Labour.

e Here is another good A-grade answer. The student has taken the four points identified and expressed them originally, with some additions to the basic comments. This is excellent technique.

(c) Firstly, we should examine what is meant by the term 'president'. Having done so, I shall investigate whether changes in the position of the prime minister do indeed amount to a presidency in effect. Finally, I shall make an overall assessment of the issue.

A president is a head of state. This means he represents the whole nation rather than just the government. He is expected to deal with crises and emergencies, to deal with military issues and to negotiate with foreign powers. There is also a presidential style. Michael Foley has described the 'British presidency'. By this he means that the British prime minister is somehow separate from the rest of government. Whatever the fortunes of the government, a president is able to separate himself and appeal directly to the people as an individual.

There have been a number of changes in the position of the British prime minister in recent years. The most important is that he has become the main spokesman for the government and deals with the media on this basis. This concentration on the prime minister by the public and the media makes him look increasingly like a president. As the passage says, the prime minister is much concerned with the presentation of policy.

Secondly, the Cabinet Office is now beginning to resemble the White House. There is a small army of advisers and a Policy Unit which serves the prime minister. There are also many private advisers and spin doctors.

The prime minister has dominated the cabinet for many years but now the cabinet hardly seems to matter at all. The meetings are shorter and it rarely discusses anything very important. In the US, the cabinet is of little importance and is completely controlled by the president. The prime minister no longer seems to be *primus inter pares* but is, as Foley says, something of a British president.

Tony Blair and Margaret Thatcher have adopted a kind of presidential style by using the media a great deal and feeding expectations that they speak for the whole of the government. When there have been crises such as the Gulf War, Kosovo, Northern Ireland or foot and mouth disease, we can see how the prime minister tries to take personal control like a president.

On balance, therefore, we can see that the prime minister is indeed virtually a president. He is not, of course, the head of state, but he often behaves like one. His style is presidential and he has many of the powers of a president.

e Another grade A is awarded. The quality of the writing is not perfect, but this is a well-constructed argument. The candidate loses a few marks for content as one or two more points could have been added, especially on foreign policy and Europe. However, there are enough marks for analysis, writing quality and content to make this a comfortable grade-A answer.

e **This good overall performance uses stimulus material effectively in answers that are carefully constructed and clearly expressed. The candidate was well prepared and is rewarded for organisation.**

Ministers and civil servants

Question 6.1

Read the following passage:

When Sir Robin Ibbs unveiled the Next Steps programme, transferring civil service functions to executive agencies, he suggested that there could be as few as 20,000 civil servants in the traditional sense of the word. The other 400,000 or so would have lost their posts owing to privatisation, be working in semi-independent agencies, or have transferred their work to one of the many advisory, regulatory and administrative bodies collectively known as quangos.

Instead there will be many servants of the state who will work within a variety of different institutions. They will have their own recruitment and promotion procedures, codes of practice, incentive schemes and internal management structure. Whether we still call them civil servants matters little. The importance of these developments lies in the fact that there will no longer be a unified civil service, the basis of which was established as long ago as 1854.

Source: *The Civil Service*, Neil McNaughton, Hodder and Stoughton, 2000.

(a) How does the passage suggest that the unified civil service has been broken up? (6 marks)

(b) What is the role of the 20,000 or so civil servants who Ibbs suggested would remain in their traditional status? (12 marks)

(c) What are the main ways in which the civil service has developed since 1979? (22 marks)

Grade-A mark scheme for question 6.1 (65%+)

(a) The passage refers to the creation of agencies instigated by Sir Robin Ibbs and the growing importance of the quangos that many civil servants have been transferred to. It also refers to the fact that the terms of employment of the civil service have changed with new recruitment and promotion procedures. Ibbs suggests as many as 400,000 civil servants could be affected by this break up. The main point to be emphasised is that the civil service used to be a unified organisation but is now being steadily split up.

(b) The core 20,000 civil servants are those who would be closely and directly concerned with policy-making as opposed to implementation and operations. Grade-A responses should include a full description of the role of the senior civil service as well as some illustrations of their work: gathering and presenting information, consulting with outside groups, developing options for policy and giving general advice. In some cases they may make administrative decisions on behalf of ministers. Examples of such delegation are planning decisions, trade licensing, immigration decisions or similar. It should be pointed out that civil servants might have special expertise and have to adapt their knowledge for use by the minister in such areas as economic policy, health decisions and education policy. All cogent examples will be credited.

(c) The various stages in reform and development should be identified and described. These are likely to include all or most of the following points: the Rayner reforms and Financial Management Initiative (FMI) of the early 1980s, which began the process of introducing business methods to the service; the Ibbs proposals; the creation of the executive agencies; the nature of these agencies; the Citizen's Charter; and market testing. Some discussion of developments under New Labour should be added, such as the principle of best value, joined-up government and other modernisation processes. There should be an overall assessment of general changes, such as managerialism, public service, private sector partnerships. Some, but not all, of these changes should be included.

Grade-B/C answer to question 6.1

(a) The civil service was broken up by Sir Robin Ibbs's creation of executive agencies in the 1980s. This meant that civil servants were no longer employed by government departments but by the new agencies. These civil servants are not responsible for policies but are only concerned with implementation. Some examples of the split-off agencies are the Benefits Agency and the Highways Agency. The employees make sure that benefits are paid and that roads are built and maintained, but do not make policy on roads or on benefits.

e The candidate deals well with one aspect of the question and has shown good technique by going beyond the text. However, the omission of other elements, notably the new promotion and recruitment, lowers the mark to a grade C.

(b) Civil servants are anonymous, neutral and permanent. This makes them very different from ministers. They are not allowed to be identified with policies and have a low public profile. They have to remain neutral so that they do not actually make policy but are only involved in policy development at early stages. They are allowed to advise ministers, but are not allowed to make political decisions.

They are also permanent, unlike ministers, who hold their positions temporarily. This means they have special experience and expertise which ministers do not have. They adopt the policies of the department and often try to impose them on ministers even though they are not supposed to.

Civil servants appear before select committees to explain policies, but they are not allowed to give any political opinions in public. They do implement policy but this is under strict orders from their ministers.

In attempting to discuss the constitutional role of civil servants rather than their political and administrative roles, the student is not answering the question asked. Most of the analysis marks are therefore lost. However, examiners think positively and try to give marks for relevant information, so some credit is given for accurate descriptions and information. Nonetheless, this is a classic case of a candidate answering the question they hoped would be asked. Here there is just enough content to scrape a grade C.

(c) There have been many changes to the civil service since 1979. I shall describe these changes and then look at what New Labour intends to do next. Finally, I shall assess the extent of these changes.

Margaret Thatcher appointed Derek Rayner of Marks and Spencer in 1979 to make the civil service more efficient and force it to adopt business methods. The efficiency meant that the numbers of civil servants fell from three quarters of a million down to half a million. Secondly, he introduced the FMI, which made the service set its own targets and monitor how it was achieving the targets.

Rayner was succeeded by Sir Robin Ibbs, who created the executive agencies, which had the role of policy implementation rather than policy-making. Some of these agencies employ thousands of civil servants. They are independent, have their own finances and are allowed to recruit people from outside. Where civil servants had once been government employees throughout their careers, now they can move in and out of the service. They also have many incentives to do a better job, to save money and to be more efficient.

John Major continued with the agencies and more were created, and New Labour has continued the policy. This brings me to the subject of New Labour and its efforts to continue with modernisation by making partnerships with the private sector plus a host of new committees and agencies dealing with areas like drugs, women and poverty.

So overall, the civil service is now smaller, more efficient and more dynamic with more incentives to do a good job. There are also many new agencies so that the civil service has been completely split up.

A borderline is awarded A/B for a well-constructed mini-essay that explains three main changes and attempts an assessment at the end. The candidate gains good — though not top — marks for powers of expression and analysis but loses on content because some of the changes have been omitted. The best answer has been saved for a predictable question in the section with the highest marks.

These answers are on the borderline between B and C. An A grade would have been in sight had the candidate answered the precise question for section (b), though a rather weak stimulus–response in section (a) was also a problem. The candidate's weakness lay in the approach to the questions in the exam room rather than in the preparation for the exam.

Question 6.2

(a) What is meant by 'civil service neutrality'? (20 marks)

(b) To what extent have recent changes eroded civil service neutrality? (20 marks)

Grade-A mark scheme for question 6.2 (65%+)

(a) A definition of neutrality should be supported by a description of the wider implications of neutrality. There will be a clear understanding of the requirements to avoid party politics and to give advice on an impartial basis within the limitations of government policy. Some illustrations will be used to underpin the explanations.

(b) The ways in which civil service reform may have eroded neutrality must be explained with illustrations. The changes include the more extensive use of temporary civil servants (private advisers), the possibilities that the ideological demands of Thatcherism and New Labour may have eroded neutrality, and the greater use of the Cabinet Office in policy-making.

■ ■ ■

Grade-A answer to question 6.2

(a) Neutrality is one of the important constitutional principles of the British civil service. Civil servants are not allowed to be involved in political activity and must also not allow their political views to be known. Opinions that they may hold must not be allowed to influence the way they give advice or the decisions they make.

When civil servants give advice, they must do so on a completely neutral basis and they are expected to serve any government of any colour with the same amount of care and enthusiasm. When they give advice they must take two things into account. The first is that they should decide what is in the national interest rather than the interests of the party in power. The second is that they are not expected to question government policy. It is important that they give ministers equal options and not try to steer them in one direction. In economic policy, for example, ministers may want tax cuts to make them more popular, but civil servants should advise what is best for the economic future of the country.

Neutrality is a vital aspect of British government. It means there is more continuity and it prevents an extreme government from promoting policies that are not in the national interests. It is also important to prevent dictatorial government. Totalitarian regimes have always controlled the civil service, but the British neutral and independent civil service promotes the national interest.

e This is a good grade-A standard, explaining the doctrine of neutrality in most of its facets by way of some useful illustrations. The student's observations about totalitarian regimes are not required but create a favourable impression in a performance that shows evidence of wide reading on the topic.

(b) The main way in which neutrality has been eroded concerns the issue of patronage. Margaret Thatcher was known to favour a certain type of civil servant and became involved in promoting her chosen officials. She often asked: 'Is he one of us?', a question which suggests she wanted civil servants who were in tune with her own ideology. Tony Blair is also interested in which civil servants are promoted and has tried to promote the New Labour project in the service.

A growth in the use of private advisers to balance out the power of the civil service has undermined neutrality. While these advisers are actually temporary civil servants, they are not expected to be neutral and, in fact, serve the government and specific ministers.

Civil servants now appear in public more often, especially the cabinet secretary. They also give evidence to select committees, where their defence of government policy further undermines strict neutrality.

Governments are now more interested in the presentation of policy. Civil servants are not supposed to do this but it is believed that some, especially in the Cabinet Office, have become involved in promoting the government and party interests. There is a fine line between serving the nation and serving the government and ruling party, and it is impossible to ensure that civil servants never cross this line. The media have to be dealt with and ministers do not have the time to do this themselves.

Despite all this, civil servants still have a good reputation for being neutral and there is little evidence that they are as 'politicised' as may have been the case under Thatcher. However, vigilance is still needed to counteract the trend towards partiality.

e This is an excellent response which discusses the points with an understanding of the issues involved. The assessment at the end is firm but balanced and could have been enhanced with illustrations, discussing maybe the role of Alastair Campbell. This is the only weakness in a solid grade-A answer.

e **A solid grade A is awarded overall. The main impression is of a candidate who is widely read and who shows good powers of expression in well-constructed answers. The weakness is in the lack of illustration.**

Question 6.3

(a) What are the main roles of a cabinet minister? (5 marks)

(b) What is the doctrine of individual ministerial responsibility? (10 marks)

(c) To what extent has the doctrine been eroded in the past 20 years?
(15 marks)

(d) How much political control can ministers exercise over the civil service?
(20 marks)

Grade-A mark scheme for question 6.3

(a) All the main functions of a cabinet minister should be included and described to the fullest extent possible within the time limitation. These should include: departmental responsibilities; collective decision-making; presentation of government policy to parliament, the media and the public; and settlement of disputes within government. Cabinet committees will be referred to.

(b) Answers need to be precise and should concentrate on the principle that ministers are responsible (accountable) for everything done by their own department. They must justify decisions, accept criticism and resign in extreme circumstances. Different views on the resignation should be briefly described. The orthodox position holds that ministers remain fully responsible and this should be contrasted with the modern position that resignation applies to errors of a very serious nature or to circumstances where the prime minister has decided a minister must go. Examples such as Lord Carrington or Sir Leon Brittan may be used. Discussion of the weakness of the doctrine should be minimised as this is the subject of section (c). The protection of the anonymity of civil servants should also be referred to.

(c) See mark scheme for question 5.1(a).

(d) Theory has it that ministers make all important political decisions and that neutral civil servants are not expected to become involved in politics. The elected, accountable nature of ministers should be contrasted with the unelected, non-accountable nature of officials, which should in turn be contrasted with the reputed influence of civil servants, with mention of such features as their permanence, expertise and their ability to influence ministers through control of information. The arguments that civil servants do indeed have influence should be clearly expounded and contrasted with the growing control the prime minister exerts over the bureaucracy. The use of private advisers to balance the power of permanent civil servants and increase government's ideological unity should also be explained.

Grade-A answer to question 6.3

(a) Cabinet ministers have a dual role with both a specific governmental brief and a role as part of a collective body. On the one hand, they have a department (where, for example, the chancellor of the exchequer runs the Treasury and the home secretary runs the Home Office), whereas other government officers, such as the leader of the

House, have a function but not a department. On the other hand, cabinet ministers form a collective body which makes and presents policy. They ratify decisions made elsewhere and also sit on sub-committees known as cabinet committees. They deal with the detail of decisions and make recommendations to the whole cabinet and the prime minister.

e The candidate was fully prepared for the question. The excellent response provides as much as could be expected in the limited time and warrants a clear grade A.

(b) The doctrine of individual ministerial responsibility has two meanings. The first is the traditional idea and the other is how it works in practice today. The traditional view is that a minister is responsible for any mistakes made in his department, whether he was involved in a decision or not. This is essential to protect the civil servants' anonymity. Resignation can follow a bad decision, as happened after the Falklands War when Lord Carrington resigned over the handling of the Argentine invasion.

The meaning today is that a minister is responsible only for those political decisions he has made himself. Decisions made by lower officials are not his concern and he need not resign. The lower official may be sacked instead. This happened when the then home secretary, Michael Howard, sacked Derek Lewis, the head of the prison service. Howard said he was not responsible for mistakes which had been made and refused to resign.

This is not the same as collective responsibility, where the whole cabinet is responsible and will resign together or defend every policy, whether they agree or not.

e Here is a fully developed grade-A response with two views well described. However, the candidate wasted time by including the final paragraph and is creating a problem because section (a) was also too long. Next come the higher-value questions and there may not be time to complete them.

(c) As I have said above, the doctrine of collective responsibility has been eroded. Michael Howard refused to resign and sacked a lower official instead. The same happened over the Scott Report about 'Arms to Iraq', when no ministers resigned. With New Labour we have had Peter Mandelson and then Lord Falconer, both of whom should have resigned over the Dome fiasco.

Ministers do not wish to take the blame these days. They tend to refuse questions in parliament and attempt to blame decisions on civil servants and other officials. So it could be said the principle has almost disappeared.

e This is a hurried answer with poorer writing, skimpier explanations and one which omits material. We have to suspect that the student knew more but could not get it down in time. The basic points are only enough to earn a grade C.

(d) The television programme *Yes Minister* showed civil servants exercising power by plotting and keeping information from the minister. It was obvious they knew more about the work of the department than the minister and so they controlled policy.

Maybe this was an exaggeration, but it was known to be partly true. Since Thatcher, the roles have been reversed.

Running out of time. Bullet points to finish.

- Thatcher brought civil service under political control
- use of private temporary civil servants like Alastair Campbell and Ed Balls who balance power of civil servants
- ministers know more and have more expert advice
- more open government so there is less secrecy
- civil servants are now very much more servants
- conclusion: constitutional position of civil servants who do have power but ministers have more control now

e As we suspected, the candidate has run out of time and, sensibly, has finished with bullet points. The answer starts well and earns credit for that, but loses marks for quality of writing and for analysis. It keeps many of the content marks for a high grade C.

e **Had this well-prepared candidate controlled the answers to (a) and (b), a grade A would have been likely. Better time management could have led to a better performance in (c) and (d), and the failure here means that a grade B goes to a student who should have done better. Here is a classic case of how an excellent candidate can underperform.**

Devolution, regional and local government

Question 7.1

Read the following passage:

Welsh devolution is a serious attempt to improve democratic control over the way in which public spending is distributed. It transfers to the region the ability to influence and improve the government of Wales in ways which are approved by those living in Wales rather than by representatives from all over the UK in the form of the Westminster parliament. It may be that pressure groups, operating in the forum of Welsh politics, will begin to concentrate their efforts on the Welsh Assembly and so have more direct influence. It may also be that the democratic control over quangos will be strengthened.

It represents a significant decentralisation of powers from London to Wales. Large quantities of public funds will be handled in Cardiff. The appointments of key officials in both government and quangos will fall into the hands of Welsh rather than English politicians. Whether devolution will lead to a stronger sense of Welsh identity remains to be seen. This is certainly the hope of Plaid Cymru, which has now adopted full independence, or at least a federal arrangement, as the centrepiece of its policy.

Source: *Local and Regional Government in Britain*, Neil McNaughton, Hodder and Stoughton, 1998.

(a) How does the passage suggest that democracy in Wales will be enhanced by devolution? (7 marks)

(b) Why does devolution not fully satisfy the demands of Plaid Cymru? (8 marks)

(c) Is it likely that devolution will lead to full independence for Wales? (10 marks)

(d) What arguments can be advanced to suggest that devolution should not have been granted to Wales? (25 marks)

Grade-A mark scheme for question 7.1 (65%+)

(a) There will be some development beyond the stimulus material, but additional issues not referred to in the passage will receive no credit. The points to be included and explained are: the distribution of government spending; the influence by the people of Wales rather than elsewhere; more opportunities for pressure groups; democratic control over quangos; decentralisation of power; and local control over patronage. All points must be included.

(b) The problem for Plaid Cymru lies in the distinction drawn between devolution, federalism and independence. Responses should point out that Plaid Cymru wishes to transfer more power to Wales, but that devolution was a limited process. The point that some members of Plaid Cymru favour full independence may be included.

(c) This response should elucidate why full independence might or might not follow devolution. All points will be credited if they are well justified by evidence. Such issues as the growth of Welsh identity, economic circumstances, the success or failure of devolved institutions, the electoral success or failure of Plaid Cymru and developments in the European Union (EU) are likely to be prominent.

(d) The range of arguments is likely to include an analysis of the referendum results, assessment of the state of Welsh national identity and culture, the expense of creating additional bureaucracy and the lack of separateness of the Welsh economy and society. Any other valid points will be acceptable and credited, if properly justified. No credit is available for arguments in favour of devolution.

■ ■ ■

Grade-A/B answer to question 7.1

(a) Six main points are raised in the passage. Firstly, it says that the people of Wales will have more say in how government expenditure is distributed in Wales. This is more democratic as the people will have a full say in such issues as health, education, transport and agriculture.

Secondly, it says that the people of Wales in general will make their own decisions rather than people elsewhere in Britain. It can be said that it is more democratic if decisions are brought closer to the people (subsidiarity).

Thirdly, it suggests that pressure groups will have a better access to the political system. Pressure groups are a vital part of democracy so anything which gives them more influence must improve democracy.

Fourthly, there will be more control of quangos. Quangos are not elected government bodies and it is important they are controlled locally rather than centrally.

Fifthly, it says that power is decentralised and this is thought to be more democratic.

Finally, there is the issue of patronage. Instead of political leaders being appointed from London, devolved government in Wales will appoint them, so there will be more democratic control over the process. This completes the points raised in the passage.

e This is a model way of answering such a question. The quality of writing is not exceptional, but it is clear and includes all the points. (The examinee probably marked or highlighted the passage before starting the answer, or possibly wrote a brief plan.) The limited development of points fitted time constraints to produce an answer that earns a high grade A.

(b) Plaid Cymru is really a Welsh nationalist party that wants full independence for Wales. Devolution does not do this because it means that limited powers are transferred and the government in London remains sovereign. Plaid Cymru wants sovereignty to be transferred to Wales. This would mean that the Welsh would have a full parliament which could pass its own laws. As things are, the Welsh Assembly cannot make primary legislation. Independence would also mean that power could not be returned to London in the future. Finally, and most importantly, Plaid Cymru wants full independence so that Wales can have a separate voice in the EU. With devolution, it is the British government which represents Wales in Brussels, and Plaid Cymru wants Wales to have a separate voice to get a good deal for Wales. For these reasons Plaid Cymru is happy to achieve devolution but now wants matters to go one stage further.

e This is a difficult answer to assess. It is an excellent discussion of devolution versus independence, which highlights the fact that many members of Plaid Cymru want full independence. However, it is not accurate to say that independence is the only alternative to devolution because there could also be a greater number of devolved powers or a federal settlement. So, marks for content are low, but there are enough marks for quality of writing and powers of analysis to bring this answer to a borderline A/B grade.

(c) I believe that devolution will lead eventually to full independence for Wales. My reasons are as follows.

First, there will be a steady growth of Welsh nationalism as the Welsh get used to the idea of governing themselves and wish to have more power. This is already happening in Scotland and is a strong force in Northern Ireland. The Welsh will see how those two countries have more freedom from London and will wish to follow. Support for the Welsh language is growing and increasing the feeling of Wales as a separate culture.

Second, it is clear that support for Plaid Cymru is growing. This is because the Welsh are dissatisfied with the performance of the English parties. This was exemplified during the farce over the choice of the Labour leader in Wales and then the collapse of the Labour executive and its replacement by the Labour/Liberal Democrat coalition. There has also been much controversy over agriculture, especially BSE and foot and mouth.

Third, Plaid Cymru policy holds that Wales should have a stronger voice in Europe in the hope that the principality could have the same success as the Republic of Ireland if it was independent. The Republic has received huge economic help from the EU and Wales would like the same.

So, for all these reasons, I believe that devolution in Wales will indeed lead to full independence in the future.

e This answer has several virtues. It is well written, each of the points is clearly explained and developed, and it has a firm conclusion which is specific to the question. However, it has one major fault, which is lack of balance. While it is acceptable that a candidate makes a strong case, there should also be an airing of the counter-arguments. This could then lead to a conclusion that, despite views to the contrary, the evidence shows that Wales will become independent. Marks are therefore lost for content, analysis and evaluation skills and a grade C is the result.

(d) The main argument for suggesting Wales should not have been granted devolution is that the Welsh did not really want it. The referendum had a 50% turnout, of whom only 51% voted for devolution. This means that 75% of the Welsh did not support devolution. Also, Plaid Cymru did not win the elections to the Welsh assembly and would surely have done better if Welsh nationalism had been strong.

Another argument is that Wales is not really a separate country. Unlike Scotland and Northern Ireland, it has never had its own government or parliament. The culture of most of Wales is very similar to England and the demands for devolution were really made by a minority of the Welsh. Labour gave devolution because it wanted to preserve its support there, not because it really believed in it.

There are a number of other arguments. The first is that devolution is very expensive in demanding another layer of government and increased bureaucracy. There was already a Welsh Office, which looked after Welsh affairs, so why have an assembly and large executive? Secondly, some people have said that it will lead to calls for the eventual break-up of the UK, a Conservative argument I do not accept.

One last point is that the Welsh will actually get a worse deal. Wales is less prosperous than England and if it loses the subsidies it enjoys, the economy will suffer.

e Here is a return to a grade-A answer, though not a high one, as the writing quality has begun to suffer in what appears to be a partially planned and rushed response. However, the candidate has addressed the question successfully and included the main points for most of the content marks. This is a good illustration of how to maintain a high mark even when short of time.

e **Overall, this response varies in quality and is strongest in the (d) section which carries half the marks. Had the candidate adjusted the answer to section (c) into a more balanced response, a comfortable grade A would have resulted. As it is, this is a borderline A/B grade, probably just making a grade A.**

Question 7.2

Study the following data:

Referendum results on Scottish devolution, 11 September 1997

Question	% in favour	% against
Do you want a Scottish Parliament established	74.3	25.7
Do you want a Scottish Parliament to have tax-varying powers?	63.5	36.5

Turnout: 61.5% of the total electorate

Referendum result on Welsh devolution, 11 September 1997

Question	% in favour	% against
Do you want a devolved government and assembly	50.3	49.7

Turnout: 51.2% of the total electorate

(a) What are the main differences in the voting figures between the two referenda? (6 marks)

(b) Comment on the differences between the questions asked in Scotland and Wales. (12 marks)

(c) What led the government to propose the introduction of devolved government in Scotland and Wales in 1997? (22 marks)

Grade-A mark scheme for question 7.2

(a) There will be discussions of the differences between the size of the Scottish and Welsh majorities and an assessment of the results. The turnout issue should be discussed with reference to the idea that the low Welsh turnout might have invalidated the result. This should be clearly contrasted with the Scottish turnout.

(b) The difference between an assembly and a parliament should be identified and explained, particularly with reference to Scottish powers to make primary legislation. Some examples should be included to illustrate this point. The issue of tax-varying powers should also be explored, including reasons why there was a difference and how taxation powers are likely to affect Scottish government and politics.

(c) A full range of political considerations should be included and explained. Most of the following should be covered: the growth of support for nationalist parties; Labour's desire to decentralise government; Labour's need to protect its electoral support in Wales and Scotland; the need to conform to EU policy on subsidiarity (as expressed at Maastricht in 1992); the need to head off demands for full independence by granting partial autonomy; the hope that Labour would be able to dominate devolved administrations and thus take political initiative away from the nationalists; an English desire to minimise subsidies to Wales and Scotland. Most, though not all, of these points should be included. Any other aspects will be credited provided they are properly justified.

■ ■ ■

Grade-C answer to question 7.2

(a) There were three votes here. Firstly, there was the main Scottish vote with its clear majority of nearly 75%. This is definitely enough to justify giving Scotland its own parliament. The second vote was to decide whether the Scottish parliament should have powers to vary taxes. This achieved only 63% support as the Scots feared that taxes would rise if they voted for it. It is a problem whether this was a big enough 'yes' vote to change the tax system. Finally, there was the Welsh vote, which was almost level. Many said the majority was not enough and that there should have been a bigger overall 'yes' vote to go ahead.

e The candidate has made a key mistake in failing to note all the stimulus material and so has omitted any discussion of turnout. This was a vital issue which differentiated the votes and had political significance. The response is clear and accurate in its conclusions but too scant for more than a grade C.

(b) The main difference in the questions put to the electorates was that the Scots were also asked if they wanted the parliament to have tax-varying powers. This meant that the level of income tax in Scotland could be varied by up to 3% higher or lower than in England. The Welsh were not given this choice because it is not considered a separate country.

The electorates had different choices in that in Scotland they were voting for or against a parliament and in Wales for an assembly. The difference in terminology is in the greater powers that a parliament has, with control, for example, over law and order, which the Welsh assembly does not have. As we have already said, the Scottish parliament also has control over some taxation while the Welsh assembly does not. However, neither the Scottish parliament nor the Welsh assembly has sovereignty.

The other main difference is that the Welsh assembly can be overruled by British government whereas the Scottish parliament cannot. It has its own powers. In other words, the Welsh assembly can be prevented from enforcing a decision which conflicts with British law. This is not the case in Scotland.

e This response can only be awarded a grade B because the candidate has not stated that a parliament's right to pass primary legislation is what distinguishes it from an assembly. The discussion on whether decisions could be overruled reveals understanding at a basic level. Better preparation would have enabled the candidate to express this key point more adequately.

(c) The main reason the Labour government promoted devolution was because it believed that this was what the people of Wales and Scotland favoured. By giving them what they wanted, they hoped to gain many votes there. This actually worked because Labour did very well in the 1997 elections in Wales and Scotland.

Another reason was that Labour was worried about the UK breaking up because of the rise of nationalism. By giving the Welsh and the Scots devolution, it hoped to fend off demands for full independence. If Labour had ignored demands for devolution, there might have been a build-up of frustration, leading to calls for greater independence.

Finally, Labour is generally in favour of regional government and believes power should be brought as close to the people as possible and devolution conformed to this agenda. Labour is also interested in regional government for parts of England and for giving more power to local government. Labour has also introduced an elected mayor for London as well as an assembly.

For these reasons, Labour introduced devolution, and to a great extent it has been successful. The data show that the people voted for it and all the institutions have been successfully set up. Labour has made itself popular in Wales and Scotland for what it has done.

e This looks like a case of under-preparation. The candidate knew only a narrow selection of the reasons for the devolution proposals instead of all of them. However, there is a good deal of content that is explained accurately and justified reasonably enough to achieve a grade C.

e **This is an example of a typical grade-C candidate who is competent, knows a good deal and can write quite well. The two main reasons why a higher grade is not achieved are: the candidate was not thorough enough in preparation and revision and needed a wider range of points to gain marks for content; inadequate response to all aspects of a question are apparent in section (a), and a vital point is missed in (b).**

Question 7.3

Study the following data:

Northern Ireland assembly elections, 1998

Party	% first preference votes	Seats gained
SDLP	22.0	24
UUP	21.3	28
DUP	18.1	20
SF	17.6	18
APNI	6.5	6
UKUP	4.5	5
Ind U	2.9	3
PUP	2.6	2
NIWC	1.6	2
Others	2.9	0
Total	**100**	**108**

Scottish parliament election, 1999

Party	Constituency contests % votes	Seats	Regional lists % votes	Seats	Total seats
Conservative	15.5	0	15.4	18	18
Labour	38.8	53	33.6	3	56
Liberal Democrat	14.2	12	12.4	5	17
Scottish Nationalist	28.7	7	27.3	28	35
Others	2.7	1	11.3	2	3

(a) The Northern Ireland elections were held using the single transferable vote system (STV). What features of STV can account for the nature of the results? (12 marks)

(b) Account for differences between the results of the constituency contests and the regional lists in the Scottish election. (20 marks)

(c) Why is proportional representation (PR) used in Scottish and Northern Ireland elections? (28 marks)

(d) What evidence is there in all the data to support the arguments for the introduction of PR for British general elections? (30 marks)

Grade-A mark scheme for question 7.3 (65%+)

(a) A full description of how STV works is not required. However, there will be a discussion of the features which have produced the results shown, including: the proportionality of the outcome; the wide range of parties represented; the number of minority groups; and the splitting of the unionist movement. The STV aspects referred to may include: the existence of multi-member constituencies; the fact that voters may place all candidates in their preferences; that there may be split-ticket voting and voters may include very small groups in their high preference; and the fact that lower preferences have an impact. Note should be made that, under first-past-the-post (FPTP), very few parties would have stood or been elected. Most, though not all, of these points should be included.

(b) Answers should explain the difference between the two sections of the election. Clear understanding should be shown of why the list elections were proportional whereas the FPTP section produced a distorted result. Full use should be made of examples from the data to illustrate these results.

(c) Answers should demonstrate an understanding of the need for PR in the two regions and why PR might be seen as a more desirable system in general. They might also discuss the notion that these elections might be seen as an experiment. Responses must show sensitivity to the different requirements in the two areas: Scottish polls needed to reflect the pluralist nature of the political system and, in particular, to reflect nationalist support; for Northern Ireland, students must refer to the need for full representation for all groups and the problem of the province's sectarian background.

(d) The range of arguments will deploy data from the tables to consider increased voter choice, the proportionality of results and the representation of smaller parties. No credit will be available for counter-arguments, which are not required in the question.

Grade-A answer to question 7.3

(a) STV is a system which does two things. Firstly, voters get a much wider choice and are able to vote for more than one candidate. Under FPTP, voters have only one choice. Secondly, it is extremely advantageous for smaller parties. We can see how many different small unionist groups were elected in this system. STV is a very proportional system so we can see that nine different parties were elected in reflection of the way many Northern Ireland constituencies are split along sectarian lines. It is important that people have more than one representative in the Northern Ireland Assembly. A Unionist would not want to be represented by a Sinn Fein member and vice versa. So STV is undoubtedly the best system for Northern Ireland.

> **e** In this comfortable grade-A answer the candidate has avoided the temptation to waste time explaining the detail of STV. The main points are identified and described, using information from the data (though not quite enough). There is a good understanding of the political circumstances of Northern Ireland from a student who has clearly read wisely on this topic.

(b) The Scottish system of election is known as the additional member system (AMS). Most members are elected by FPTP which means the Labour Party has a great advantage because of its concentrated support. The Scottish Nationalist Party (SNP), the Conservatives and the Liberal Democrats do badly under FPTP for the same reasons. For example, the Scottish Nationalists won only seven seats on a 28% vote in constituencies, but won 35 seats in the list system. The Conservatives won 15% of the vote, but won no seats at all because its support is too spread out. However, under the regional list top-up system the Conservatives and Liberal Democrats do better. The Conservatives won 18 seats and the Liberal Democrats 18. This is because the list system is very proportional.

The way in which the top-up system works also favours those parties that do worse in the constituency system. They get even more regional list seats and this helped the Conservatives in particular. These very different systems produce very different results.

> **e** Here is another grade-A answer, which reveals an understanding of the system and how it affects the parties. Above all, the candidate uses the data to show how the results vary and demonstrates detailed knowledge about the top-up system.

(c) It is probably true that New Labour used these elections to experiment in the use of PR and the results prove that both AMS and STV give a fair representation to smaller parties. They create a pluralist system to more accurately reflect the political situation.

The two countries used different systems. In Scotland the main problem was the SNP and we can see how badly it would have done under FPTP. It would have won very few seats compared to the large number won under the lists. If this had happened, the SNP would have seen the system as totally unfair and this might have created anger and frustration. It was important to give the SNP a fair number of seats and the system succeeded in doing this.

In Northern Ireland it was vital to give all parties a fair share of the vote. Under FPTP the Unionists would have won such a big majority that it would have destroyed the peace process. Northern Ireland's power-sharing assembly and executive had to be proportional to ensure that all large groups won seats and could be represented. STV does preserve constituencies, unlike the list system used in Israel or Holland. This is an important issue in Ulster, so STV was ideal. It gave a proportional result, but kept constituencies.

We can now see that these two systems were carefully thought out and delivered results to suit the political situations of the two countries.

e This is another grade-A answer with several virtues to bring it close to full marks. It addresses the question fully, shows excellent knowledge of the two systems, is well written and moves toward a solid summary.

(d) FPTP favours the large parties. Either the Tories or Labour always win an overall majority (with one exception in 1974). Winning far fewer seats than they deserve has discriminated against the Liberal Democrats and the various nationalist parties. FPTP is also very unfair to voters. It gives unequal value to votes because votes in safe seats are wasted, while those in marginal seats are more valuable. A vote for a small party is also worth much less than a vote for a major party.

The data show how these problems can be overcome. In both systems the smaller parties get a much fairer number of seats. STV gives voters plenty of choice. This explains why so many smaller parties won seats. In the case of Northern Ireland there has to be power-sharing. This may be seen as a good thing as it leads to consensus politics and no single party can dominate the system, as occurs in the rest of Britain. In Scotland too Labour did not win an overall majority and so had to form a coalition. Again, this takes away undeserved power from a single dominant party.

If we introduced STV into Britain, more parties would gain seats. This can be seen as fair as they do have a good deal of support. The Scottish system would be ideal because it preserves constituencies and yet is fair in how it distributes seats. The Liberal Democrats would win enough seats to share power as they do in Scotland. This would be a desirable development as it would act as a moderation on government.

e The student has maintained a high standard and achieves another grade A, though the use of data could have been more extensive. Information has been well deployed by a candidate who has stuck to the demands of the question.

e **Overall, this is a consistent grade-A effort, which shows knowledge, technique, effective use of time and the ability to keep to the questions.**

The constitution and constitutional reform

Question 8.1

Read the following passage:

New Labour's programme of constitutional reforms was developed during the 1990s and formed a central part of the 1997 manifesto commitments. There were four identifiable themes.

- The modernisation of political institutions. The main candidates have been both Houses of Parliament, the civil service and local government.
- Greater democratisation of the political system. In particular this has been directed at increased popular participation in institutions and the decision-making process. The acceptance of the use of referendums and other forms of direct democracy are the principal initiatives, but there has also been some movement towards electoral reform and a number of other, less heralded proposals.
- The decentralisation of power from Westminster and Whitehall. Of course, devolution was at the forefront of this process, but there has also been talk of greater powers for local government and even the introduction of regional government in England.
- Improving and safeguarding individual and minority rights. The flagship for this has been the Human Rights Act which came into force on 2 October, 2001.

Source: 'Constitutional reform in the UK', Neil McNaughton, *Talking Politics*, Vol. 10, No. 4, April 2001.

(a) **What were the main effects of the Human Rights Act, introduced in October 2001?** (6 marks)

(b) **Briefly describe the main proposals for the modernisation of parliament.** (12 marks)

(c) **Briefly describe the measures, introduced since 1997, which have improved democracy in the United Kingdom.** (22 marks)

Grade-A mark scheme for question 8.1

(a) There will be a description of how the Human Rights Act will work. This will include the way it is binding on executive decisions but not Acts of Parliament. There will be knowledge shown that the courts will be able to cancel decisions that offend the European Convention. Some of the main rights described in the Convention will be covered. These are likely to include rights to expression, movement and association, the right to privacy and freedom of religion. Equality for all religious, ethnic and national groups is an important provision. The basic operation of the Act will be described, in particular its jurisdiction and the fact that while it does not bind primary legislation in parliament, it does bind other public bodies.

(b) Answers will describe the basic proposals for change in both the Lords and the Commons. Reform of the Lords will include both the current changes in terms of composition and the ideas put forward by Lord Wakeham. In the case of the Commons there will be a discussion of such possibilities as streamlining procedures, improving committees, providing more research facilities and reducing sitting hours. Any proposed reforms will be given credit.

(c) A selection of reforms concerned with democracy will be identified, such as electoral reform, decentralisation of power, local government or transfer of powers to local government, use of referenda, improvement in the protection of rights, and reform of the membership of the Lords. There may be one or two omissions, but most of the main reforms will be included.

■ ■ ■

Grade-B answer to question 8.1

(a) The Human Rights Act was a way of bringing the European Convention on Human Rights into force. The Convention contains a wide range of rights such as freedom of movement, freedom of worship and freedom of association. It prevents the government and local government from abusing people's rights. In the past the UK has had an unwritten constitution and so our rights were vulnerable. The only area where the Convention has no effect is in parliament. Parliament is sovereign in the UK and it cannot be limited by a bill of rights. Ministers, civil servants and members of local councils will have to take into account the terms of the Human Rights Act. The courts will enforce it if they think that something or somebody has broken the Act.

e This answer is basically accurate but could have developed information about the terms of the bodies which must conform to the act, notably the devolved assemblies. The candidate is strong in the treatment of parliamentary sovereignty and would just make a grade A.

(b) I shall discuss first the proposals for reform of the House of Lords and then deal with the House of Commons.

The House of Lords is a traditional body that needs modernising. The Labour government has already removed most of the hereditary peers (leaving just 92) and it is likely that the rest will go soon. It has also appointed more life peers, many of whom are experts in their fields and can represent many groups in society. There are more women and people from varied backgrounds.

Although the powers of the Lords will probably stay unchanged, the Wakeham report proposed that about one third of peers should be elected and that appointments should be controlled carefully.

The House of Commons is elected and so is more modern. However, it has old-fashioned procedures and MPs have little power. There are ideas to extend research facilities with a new building for MPs providing better offices for all of them. They want to have stronger committees and the hours of work to be improved so that more women are willing to take part.

Generally, parliament will never be truly modern as long as it has such limited power. Neither house is representative and we need to change the electoral system accordingly.

e This is only just a grade A. There could be more development of proposals for both houses, especially the Commons. The examinee does not give much detail about proposals to improve the work of Commons' committees but does cover the main points with accurate descriptions.

(c) There are a number of proposals for constitutional change to improve democracy in the UK. We need to define democracy as follows: people should be free and have rights protected, there should be free and fair elections, equal rights and everybody should be able to participate freely in the political system. We can now look at the reforms to see which of them improve democracy.

The main item is electoral reform, which has already happened in Scotland and Wales. There may be more electoral reform embodying positive ideas in the Human Rights and Freedom of Information Acts.

Devolution has been good for democracy, especially in Scotland and Wales. The reform of the House of Lords means that it is more democratic, but it will not be fully democratic until it is an elected chamber.

Finally, there are now more referenda, which are an example of direct democracy. There may be more of these, especially over the introduction of the single European currency.

e This response is not as good as the first two parts and is worth a grade B. The points are not well developed. The candidate was probably running out of time. There are also one or two omissions, such as local government reform and regional devolution.

e **The candidate's weakest performance is for the section which carries the most marks. The modest grade-A responses for (a) and (b) are offset by a grade B in the final part for an overall grade B.**

■ ■ ■

Question 8.2

(a) What are the main functions of a constitution? (5 marks)

(b) What are the main sources of the British constitution? (10 marks)

(c) To what extent can it be said that British government is constitutional government? (15 marks)

(d) Distinguish between a typical Conservative and a typical Liberal attitude to the British constitution. (20 marks)

Grade-A mark scheme for question 8.2 (65%+)

(a) Answers should include all or most of the following functions: distributing power within the system; establishing the rights of the people; limiting the power of government; establishing the nature of the territory; sovereignty and citizenship.

(b) Examples should be used to illustrate all the sources of the British constitution, which should include: parliamentary statutes; European treaties; conventions; common law and judicial precedent; books of authority; customs and practices; constitutional documents.

(c) The term 'constitutional government' should be correctly explained and should include ideas that government is limited by constitutional rules, that the rule of law prevails, that power is divided and separated by entrenched rules and that the rights of the people are guaranteed. The issue of Britain's uncodified constitution and the sovereignty of parliament will be discussed in relation to constitutionalism. The status of the Human Rights Act, devolution legislation and European agreements will also be included.

(d) The Conservative view is of an organic, flexible constitution which reflects a balance between democratic and traditional elements. This will be distinguished from the Liberal view, which stresses limited government, entrenchment, guaranteed rights and the separation of powers. The Liberal view would also reflect democratic principles as opposed to traditional elements. The two views will be extensively illustrated.

■ ■ ■

Grade-D answer to question 8.2

(a) A constitution is really a set of rules, like the laws of the game of cricket or football. It sets out how government should be organised, who has powers over what and how the processes work. A constitution also demonstrates the relationship between the people and the state. It is a bit like a contract between government and the governed. Britain does not really have a constitution, so the rules of things like how parliament works, how ministers are chosen or the powers of the prime minister are vague. The US has a written constitution which shows the power of the president, the congress and the courts.

> e A grade C is awarded to a candidate who knows what a constitution is and has described some of its functions accurately. However, other functions are omitted or the explanations are weak and unspecific. There are a good number of marks for understanding, but few for powers of expression. The style is too informal. This student needed to be better prepared and to have learned a formal set of functions.

(b) The British constitution comes from a whole series of different sources. Conventions are the unwritten rules, such as how the prime minister chooses a cabinet, and these are the main parts of the constitution. There are also unwritten common laws which are enforced by the judges dealing with things like marriage and inheritance. These tell us about our rights. We must remember too the European arrangements and how sovereignty is divided between Britain and Europe. There are also books of authority like Bagehot's *English Constitution* and Blackstone's *Commentaries*. There are ancient documents as well, such as *Magna Carta,* which deals with rights. So we can see the British constitution is partly written and is partly conventional.

e The candidate has omitted any mention of the importance of statutes and is not up to date with knowledge of the Human Rights Act or devolution arrangements. This suggests lack of preparation. It is essential to use illustrations from recent political life. This is a grade-D answer.

(c) The question here is whether Britain has a constitution or not. It is clear that we do not. A constitution is a document setting out how government works and the relationship between the people and the government. Britain has no such constitution. Instead we have a whole series of unwritten rules and conventions.

To establish what a constitution is we need to look at the US, which has a single document superior to all other laws. If a law conflicts with the constitution, the Supreme Court will set it aside. This makes the constitution superior. By contrast the courts cannot stop what parliament does. This is because we have no constitution which is superior.

The sovereignty of parliament means that there is no real limit to what government can do. A constitution would do this, but we do not have one. The answer to the question of whether we have constitutional government must be 'no'. We do have some laws and conventions which form part of a constitution, but all of these can be overturned by parliament. This means that even if we believe we have a constitution, we do not. It has been said that for us parliamentary sovereignty replaces a constitution.

e A grade C is awarded for a limited response which is saved by a good discussion of the role of parliamentary sovereignty at the end. The answer is unbalanced as it should discuss the possibility that Britain has constitutional government even in the absence of a codified constitution. The term 'constitutionalism' is not explained directly, although an implicit understanding is shown.

(d) Conservatives don't believe in a constitution at all. They believe in strong government and the use of traditional institutions. This means they accept the role of the monarchy, the hereditary peers and the sovereignty of parliament. They argue that a constitution is too rigid and gives too much power to the individual people and to the law courts which have to interpret the constitution.

Conservatives believe in a natural order in society and a constitution denies this as it makes everybody equal. It also places too many limits on the power of the monarchy and the government. They believe in traditions and the paternalism that government knows best. A constitution would mean that the people would have too much say in how they are governed. Conservatives do not believe that people know how to govern themselves.

Liberal belief in a constitution stems from a belief in the rights of the people and a rejection of ideas about traditional power. So they would limit the power of the monarchy and the government with a bill of rights. They also believe that everybody should be equal and that a constitution can achieve this.

In conclusion, the main difference is that Conservatives want things to stay as they are, with no constitution, while Liberals want us to write a constitution and take away all forms of traditional power.

e There are a few good points here concerning traditional authority, political equality and popular rights from a candidate with some idea about differences between Conservative and Liberal attitudes. However, there are gaps in an analysis which considers the issues from a basic and unsubtle point of view. The views on conservatism are outmoded and there may have been basic problems in keeping up to date with reading throughout the course. Only a grade D can be awarded.

e **This poorly prepared grade-D response reveals a candidate who may well have been lax throughout the course. However, this student at least tried to address the questions and applied a limited range of knowledge quite well.**

Question 8.3

(a) To what extent is it true to say that Britain's constitution is unwritten? (20 marks)

(b) What are the main arguments in favour of introducing a codified, entrenched constitution in Britain? (20 marks)

Grade-A mark scheme for question 8.3 (65%+)

(a) Responses will distinguish between a written and a codified constitution. The written parts to describe and illustrate are statutes, external agreements, constitutional documents and works of authority. In contrast, the codified parts of the constitution are the nature of conventions, customs and practices and common law. There will be strong knowledge of recent developments, such as the Human Rights Act, devolution and European Union (EU) agreements. There will be some degree of assessment of constitutional approaches.

(b) The arguments for codification will include such issues as clarity, control of government and better judicial control of the constitution. The term 'entrenchment' will be explained and the issues concerning entrenchment will be well explored and centre on the problems of parliamentary sovereignty. Reasons in favour of entrenchment will be explained and most will be identified. No credit is available for arguments against entrenchment.

Grade-A answer to question 8.3

(a) The answer to this question is basically that most of the British constitution is now written. It is not codified in that it has never been written in a single document in an organised way, as in the US, but this is not the same as being unwritten. Many parts are written. There are, for example, many parliamentary statutes which we can all view and understand. There is the Parliament Act which specifies the powers of the House of Lords, the Representation of the People Act which deals with voting and elections, and the devolution acts which grant powers to governments in Scotland, Wales and Northern Ireland. There are treaties and agreements with the EU which deal with how sovereignty is divided between Britain and Europe. The Maastricht Treaty is a good example of this. We also have many works of authority such as Bagehot's *English Constitution*. Finally, we now have the European Convention on Human Rights which is part of British law through the Human Rights Act.

The true question is whether the constitution is codified or not. If we ask whether it is codified, the answer is 'no'. There are also many unwritten parts. Conventions are unwritten rules, mainly dealing with the powers of the prime minister. There are a number of customs and practices which deal with the way parliament, government and the civil service behave. There is common law too although most of the common law rights have been replaced by the Human Rights Act. However, the written sections are gradually replacing the unwritten parts of the constitution. As yet it is not codified and that would be a very big step to take. A codified constitution would be clearer than the current situation. We would know who has what powers.

e This is an excellent answer and a high grade A because the candidate has done everything required by the mark scheme — differentiated clearly between codified and written, described and assessed the degree to which the constitution is written or unwritten, given examples and included a reasonable number of elements within the time constraints.

(b) Before answering this question, it is necessary to define and understand entrenchment and codification. Having established this, we can determine whether they are a reasonable option for Britain.

Codification means the writing of the constitution into a single document as the Americans did in 1787 when they had gained independence. If we did this in Britain, it would tidy up the unclear and unwritten sections of the constitution, such as the conventions, common law, customs etc. Examples are the powers of the prime minister, ministerial responsibility and the role of the civil service. Some have defined this as little more than a housekeeping exercise, but it would make our constitution clearer and, for example, describe exactly the powers of the monarchy.

Entrenchment is a much more important concept. This makes a constitution difficult to change and protects it from being altered by a future parliament. As things are, we have the sovereignty of parliament, which means that it is not possible to bind a future parliament to any constitutional principles. With an entrenched constitution, future parliaments are bound. This would be a good thing in that it would protect the rights of citizens from laws that threaten individual rights. If we take the Criminal Justice Act as an example, we can see the dangers of parliamentary sovereignty. It would also help to limit the powers of the government itself.

Insisting on referenda to make constitutional change might create entrenchment. In a sense we have already done this with devolution and the elected London mayor. Referenda involve the people and so might be a step towards more democracy. The US has a long, complicated and cumbersome legal system and this may be an argument against entrenchment.

On the other hand, if we had a codified and entrenched constitution, it would put a great deal of power into the hands of the judges. This is because they would be called on to interpret the constitution. At the moment this is done by parliament. Parliament is elected and accountable, but the judges are not. So this would be a dangerous development.

e Once again this a grade-A response. The candidate has shown knowledge of the important constitutional principles, but could have used a little more illustration. There are some unnecessary sections arguing against entrenchment and codification, which the question does not ask for — no marks gained and time wasted. A conclusion to assess the strength of the arguments would have bolstered an answer which is not quite as good as the answer to section (a).

e **Overall, this is a clear grade-A response. The candidate knows the detail, writes well and focuses on the question directly. There could possibly have been more illustrations, but there are enough here to merit a top grade.**

Rights and the judiciary

Question 9.1

(a) What is the importance of the Human Rights Act? (20 marks)

(b) What is the role of the judiciary in British politics? (20 marks)

Grade-A mark scheme for question 9.1 (65%+)

(a) The nature of the Human Rights Act will be identified and its relationship to the European Convention described along with the main rights contained in the Convention. The significance of the operation of the act will be explored, including its jurisdiction in terms of government, devolved assemblies, local government and other public bodies. Its relationship to Westminster legislation will also be described.

(b) The various ways in which the judiciary is involved in political cases will be identified, including cases concerned with *ultra vires*, judicial review, common law cases and, in the future, cases involving the Human Rights Act. The nature of the way in which the judiciary interprets laws will be described and examples offered.

■ ■ ■

Grade-A answer to question 9.1

(a) The Human Rights Act was passed in 2001 and is now effective in the UK. The act has the effect of incorporating the European Convention on Human Rights into British law. The Convention deals with rights such as freedom of movement, expression and association. It also helps to guarantee privacy, guarantees freedom of religion and freedom from racial discrimination. The convention is binding on all public bodies, including the devolved assemblies in Scotland, Wales and Northern Ireland. It also bonds local authorities and government ministers.

The way it will work is this: any laws passed by parliament do not have to meet the requirements of the act, but if so a minister has to declare this fact and parliament may then vote against the act. However, anybody may appeal against any other decision on the grounds that it is against the act. In these cases they will appeal to judges to overturn a decision. We no longer have to go to the European court as any British court will hear a case.

The importance of the act is that it might prevent government from abusing our rights. Ministers and civil servants will have to be careful in case a decision or a proposed law offends the act. In this way the cause of human rights will be much advanced in Britain. We have no bill of rights like the US or France, but now we do have a set of rights to protect us.

This solid grade-A response to a question which often appears on exam papers shows a well-prepared candidate who focused on all aspects of the question. A good number of examples are used and a nice comparison is made with France and the US.

(b) When the Human Rights Act really gets going, judges will be involved in political cases. For example, they may consider laws which extend police powers, or which limit freedom of the press. Although they cannot set them aside, they will be able to criticise the government.

The judiciary already has a great range of political powers. It can undertake judicial reviews which allow them to reverse official decisions by saying that they were against natural justice, or that a minister exceeded his powers. This happened a number of times to Michael Howard over prison procedures.

Judges hear a lot of cases that involve human rights and can try to enforce them. Newspapers may appeal if the government wants to oppress them. There have also been many cases where individuals appeal against planning decisions, tax demands or rights concerning welfare benefits.

So we can see that the judges are often involved in human rights, the powers of government and the actions of many public bodies. In this way they are involved in political issues.

A low grade A is awarded for an answer which has good examples but has a lack of scope in that there are many types of judicial review and the issue of *ultra vires* is not fully explored. However, it is well written and the points made are accurate.

The candidate has done a good job in handling a tricky question by virtue of being prepared and learning examples and illustrations. The answers may not be developed fully, but there is enough here to ensure a high grade.

■ ■ ■

Question 9.2

Read the following passage:

The Human Rights Act, which incorporates most of the European Convention on Human Rights, represents perhaps the most important advance in the United Kingdom's constitutional development since the Great Reform Act of 1832. For the first time Britain has a codified set of rights against which we can judge legislation, executive action and a host of other circumstances. Furthermore, British citizens no longer have to face the expense and delay involved in taking a case concerning our rights to the European Court of Human Rights. They can now make a claim in the British courts and decisions are likely to be reached within a relatively short period of time.

Yet, for all that, the changes may not turn out to be as dramatic as they first seem. Most of the rights contained in the Convention already exist in UK statutes or in common law. Furthermore, it has to be remembered that parliament remains legally sovereign. A determined-enough government, which feels it has a mandate to set aside one of the rights contained in the Convention, can do so if it can persuade parliament to back it. In such circumstances, there is nothing the judiciary can do about it except to draw the public attention to the facts.

Original material

(a) **In what ways does the sovereignty of parliament affect the operation of the Human Rights Act?** (6 marks)

(b) **In what circumstances is the Human Rights Act likely to involve the judiciary in politics?** (12 marks)

(c) **From the information in the passage and your own knowledge, assess the extent to which the Human Rights Act will protect individual rights.** (22 marks)

Grade-A mark scheme for question 9.2 (65%+)

(a) Answers will assert that the Human Rights Act does not extend to primary parliamentary legislation, although ministers must still make a declaration if a proposed act will break one of the provisions of the European Convention on Human Rights. Judges may also make such a declaration after the act has been passed. It will therefore be noted that legal sovereignty is not affected. The strongest responses could discuss the possibility that parliament may, nevertheless, be constrained by the Human Rights Act.

(b) There will be a clear understanding that appeals based on the act will require interpretation by the judiciary. The political significance of some cases should be noted. Examples will be used to illustrate the circumstances. These will describe cases of political importance involving the act which have taken place, or might in the future, take place. The fact that the judges' interpretations may have political significance will be clearly understood.

(c) The relevant information from the passage will be identified and include the fact that the process of appealing on a rights issue will be cheaper and quicker than the use of the European Court of Human Rights. Strong responses may suggest that the passage implies that parliament may enforce the act against the government. Other points might include: protection of individuals against excessive powers by law enforcement agencies; protected freedom of the press; increased racial protection; better protection of personal privacy; and freedom from gender discrimination. It may be pointed out, as the passage argues, that many of these rights are already well protected. Any other examples of extensions in rights will be credited, if accurately identified.

Grade-B answer to question 9.2

(a) The Human Rights Act is a list of rights brought into British law from Europe. These rights clash with the sovereignty of parliament because sovereignty means that there is nothing that can bind our parliament. But the Human Rights Act tries to do this. It may be possible for parliament to defy the act, but only if the judges allow them to do this. So the sovereignty of parliament is affected by the act, but this does not mean that the situation will change. Parliament could also repeal the act in the future so it is not bound forever. Sovereignty means that no parliament can bind its successors, so the fact that the present parliament has passed the act does not mean that future parliaments will have to obey it.

e This provides a mixed picture, which includes some sophisticated comments to the effect that future parliaments will be sovereign and so could repeal the Human Rights Act. However, the student is muddled about the jurisdiction of the act because the answer implies that judges can decide whether parliamentary legislation defies the Convention. This is a major error because the act does not extend to primary legislation and the grade, therefore, drops to a borderline B/C.

(b) The role of the judiciary is to interpret the laws. In cases where the Human Rights Act is involved, judges may have to decide what the act means. For example, when are the newspapers allowed to invade people's privacy? The judges would have to decide what privacy really means. Another kind of case would be where a woman feels she is being discriminated against by an employer and not getting equal pay. The judges would have to decide what is meant by equal pay.

These kinds of cases would hit the headlines and judges would suddenly become major figures. We might also have the situation where parliament wants to break the terms of the act and the judiciary will have to decide whether this is permissible. What if parliament wanted to give more powers to the police to search people or question them? The courts would have to decide.

Judges are not elected and not very representative, so there is a serious case as to whether they should be allowed to make such decisions. Political issues should be left to elected politicians, who are accountable. The Human Rights Act will throw judges into politics by making them give important interpretations of our rights.

e This is another mixed bag where the student has a general idea of the role of judges and understands that the act will put more important cases their way. The examples are valid and well described. However, the misunderstanding of the judiciary's role in primary legislation remains. Once again, this candidate is in error in suggesting judges decide whether parliament can break the terms of the act. The student also drifts into answering a different question at the end by discussing judges' fitness to hear important cases. Therefore, a good deal of the answer is irrelevant or inaccurate and there is only enough valid information for a grade C.

(c) The passage says clearly that the Human Rights Act is a huge step forward in protecting rights, as great as the extension of the franchise in 1832. Furthermore, cases will be dealt with more quickly than with the European Convention on Human Rights. It is bound to be cheaper because citizens will not have to go abroad to obtain justice. It also says that most of the rights already exist, so perhaps the act is not such a big step forward. But it will make a difference in dealing with a range of rights, such as:

- the right to life
- the right to family life
- freedom of movement, association and expression
- freedom from discrimination on grounds of race or religion
- the right to privacy
- the right to a fair trial
- the right to be treated equally

All these matters can now be protected in the British courts. It is also true that all political bodies must protect the rights or risk having to change a decision or pay compensation. My conclusion is that the passage is right. The Human Rights Act does not do as much as it seems. This is because parliament remains sovereign and because most of these rights already exist.

e This is a better section than the previous two, and there are no serious errors. It reaches a firm conclusion, which addresses the question 'assess the extent', and this shows good technique. The bullet point list is not a good idea: except when time is very short, prose should be used. The examples of rights are accurate, although two or three of them could have been more fully described. The examinee has not described the full extent of the act's jurisdiction, for example to devolved assemblies and local authorities. The grade is therefore a B.

e **Achieving a B grade for the section with most marks boosts the result to a grade B overall. The main problem is that the candidate has not fully understood how the Human Rights Act works and is muddled over its relationship to parliament. It is a good idea to practise describing the basic points of topical issues so that lack of clarity does not creep in, as has happened here.**

■ ■ ■

Question 9.3

(a) What is meant by 'independence of the judiciary'? (5 marks)

(b) How is judicial independence maintained? (10 marks)

(c) In what ways can the judiciary protect the rights of individuals and minorities? (15 marks)

(d) How effectively can the judiciary protect rights? (20 marks)

Grade-A mark scheme for question 9.3 (65%+)

(a) There must be a clear explanation of what independence of the judiciary means and how it is applied to the separation of powers, and of the importance of judicial independence in constitutional and political matters. The role of the judiciary will be either explicitly or implicitly included. The importance of the system of appointments will be discussed briefly.

(b) This should discuss the way in which judges are appointed and allude to the possibility of political interference. The security of tenure of judges will be mentioned, along with the regulations about the selection of judges in particular cases. The conventions governing political interference will also be included.

(c) The four main elements of rights protection should be discussed as follows. (1) The European Convention and Human Rights Act dimensions must be included at this level. In each case there will be a full description and some form of illustration within the time constraints. (2) Included will be the process of judicial review (with examples of the types of cases heard), cases of *ultra vires* (again with some illustration), (3) cases where common law or European Convention rights may be upheld and, finally, (4) the European dimension. Should either *ultra vires* or judicial review cases be omitted, the rest of the response must be very strong for a grade A to be awarded. Note that the question does not refer specifically to the British judiciary.

(d) Responses need not describe the methods of rights protection as these are included in section (c). However, most, if not the full range, of methods should be discussed. The lack of enforcement powers of the judiciary should be discussed, as well as the implications for parliamentary sovereignty. The precise jurisdiction of the Human Rights Act and its limitations should be explained and general problems related to common law and judicial review discussed. There should be a clear assessment of how successful the judiciary can be in this field.

Grade-B answer to question 9.3

(a) The French philosopher Montesquieu introduced the idea of the separation of powers as an important part of representative government. What he meant was that government had to be divided into different branches that could exert control on the others. The three branches are the executive, the legislature and the judiciary. The judiciary in Britain has to be separate and independent because there is so much power in the hands of the executive branch. What independence means is that the government cannot interfere with decisions the judiciary makes. Sometimes the judiciary has to make decisions of political importance, such as cases involving the powers of ministers or the rights of the people, for example against the police. If the government was able to control the judiciary, the people would lose their protection and this would be a serious development.

So, in conclusion, the independence of the judiciary means that politicians cannot interfere with judges. This means judges will take a neutral position in cases about the relations between the people and the government. Judges also must not be members of a political party or express political views. They should not just be independent, they must be seen to be independent.

e Although this answer has some problems, it does meet the requirements for a grade A. However, the candidate has spent too much time on this section. There is too much unnecessary detail about the philosophy of the separation of powers. It was worth mentioning, but not in this depth. The candidate has described independence of the judiciary correctly, but not concisely. Better revision preparation is called for in reducing descriptions to the essentials.

(b) The independence of the judiciary is maintained in two ways. Firstly, judges cannot be removed except for misconduct. In other words, they cannot be threatened with losing their post if they do not produce verdicts which please the government. When citizens, for example, are challenging the government for their rights, as in the Government Communications Headquarters (GCHQ) union's case against Margaret Thatcher, it is important that the decision of the judges is a neutral one. Secondly, parliament and ministers are not allowed to interfere directly in cases. In other words, they are not allowed to put any pressure on judges while the case is going on.

Unfortunately, the lord chancellor and the prime minister appoint the judges. Both are members of the government so there is a possibility that they are not really independent. If party politicians choose judges, it cannot be said that they are independent. This happens in the US and we can see that the Supreme Court is definitely not independent. Look what happened in the case of the Florida election.

e This is a more solid grade-A response because the question has been answered concisely. The candidate has clearly demonstrated that two main points are being made. The GCHQ illustration is a little dated, but relevant. Possibly there is too much information at the end, but the allusion to the US is useful.

(c) The main way in which the judges protect rights is as follows: when there is a statute which deals with the rights of citizens (such as the Human Rights Act or the Criminal Justice Act), there may be some cases of appeal concerning the statute. In such cases, the judges will have to undertake a review of the statute. When they make a judgement, the government has to follow the decision.

Examples of these cases are when prisoners have been denied their rights — maybe to speak to a solicitor or to apply for parole — and look at the laws about how they should be treated. A newspaper might also appeal, were the government to try and prevent it publishing a story. This might be a case under the Human Rights Act or even under unwritten common law.

e Having done well on the descriptive sections of this question, the standard drops to a grade D. This part required a fuller answer than the superficial consideration of the principle of judicial review. The candidate omitted to look at any of the range of devices.

(d) The question of whether the judiciary protects our rights effectively is a mixed one. In some ways it does extremely well, but there are also weaknesses. I shall discuss each in turn and make a final assessment of its effectiveness.

Since the passage of the Human Rights Act, the judiciary has been given many more powers to protect rights. We now have guarantees of rights such as freedom of expression, freedom of movement, privacy and family life. If any public body threatens these rights, we may ask for a judicial review and the judges can order a change. This did not happen before 1999.

There are also cases which can be reviewed if we think that a local authority or a minister has overstepped powers in such a way that our rights are in danger. Here the judges can order that a decision is reversed. Michael Howard was forced to change 17 decisions when he was Home Secretary. This shows how judges can actually overrule a government minister.

We must not forget that parliament is sovereign. This means that if it passes a statute which is against the Human Rights Act, there is nothing the courts can do about it. This is because parliament is superior to the Human Rights Act. This is a very great weakness for the judiciary.

We must also remember that many attempts at judicial review fail. This is mainly because the powers given to public bodies are very great. Even if the judges think they have too much power, there is nothing they can do about it. It is also true that some common law (unwritten) rights are vague and therefore difficult to enforce.

The overall picture is mixed. Judges do have great powers, especially under the Human Rights Act, but they cannot overrule parliament and many of our rights remain rather vague. The judiciary cannot enforce rights against the will of a determined parliament.

e This response is on the borderline between A and B. Its strength is in its understanding of the relevance of parliament's sovereignty and the importance of the Human Rights Act. However, there are omissions. Europe is not mentioned and there is an underestimation of the Human Rights Act in that it does control devolved government, local authorities and many public bodies. The conclusion addresses the question, which is a strength, but there is insufficient illustration.

e **Overall, these are a mixed set of responses, adding up to a grade B. The candidate may have been running out of time and the resulting weakness of section (c) stood in the way of a modest grade-A mark. Had this student been able to limit section (a) and extend section (c), the result would have been improved. Preparation and execution of answers should be more even.**

Britain and the European Union

Question 10.1

Read the following extract:

The sovereignty issue has become the main fault-line in the Conservative Party. Eurosceptics oppose further transfers of sovereignty and the erosion of the national veto, whereas pro-Europeans argue that pooling sovereignty in the European Union (EU) can increase British interests. Eurosceptics favour an association of cooperating nation-states with free trade but little else. They want to 'repatriate' policy competencies (e.g. agriculture) and weaken supranational institutions. Principled opposition to European Monetary Union (EMU) and concern about John Major's pragmatic stance unites neo-liberal and constitutionalist Eurosceptics.

Whereas John Major sought to defend British interests through negotiations at Maastricht and later claimed that British views were winning support in the EU, Eurosceptics argue that the Franco-German partnership is driving the EU towards further integration.

Source: 'British politics and European integration', Philip Lynch, *Politics Review,* Vol. 6, No. 4, April 1997.

(a) What is meant by the term 'Eurosceptic'? (7 marks)

(b) What does the extract say about how British sovereignty is affected by European integration? (8 marks)

(c) What are the main government responsibilities which have been transferred to the EU? (10 marks)

(d) From information in the extract and your own knowledge, why do many Conservatives oppose British participation in EMU? (25 marks)

Grade-A mark scheme for question 10.1

(a) A description of Euroscepticism will go beyond simple opposition to the EU and refer to opposition to further transfers of sovereignty, the undemocratic nature of the EU arrangements and fear of a federal outcome. Other relevant descriptions will be credited.

(b) Answers must allude both to the belief that the British veto is being undermined and to the view that integration involves the pooling of sovereignty. The passage implies that loss of competencies is involved and that loss of sovereignty should be confined to trade.

(c) A comprehensive group of responsibilities will be accurately identified and described briefly. These are likely to include such examples as trade, agriculture (CAP), environmental protection, employment protection and consumer protection. There will be a brief explanation of each. Other examples, provided they are accurately identified, will be credited. Some prominent examples may also be omitted.

(d) An understanding will be shown of what monetary union implies. A brief description of the system should be included, either implicitly or explicitly. The possible undesirable effects of EMU should be accurately described, including loss of national control over public finance, interest rates, economic policy and some taxation. While a basic understanding of the way monetary union involves such losses of sovereignty is necessary, no economic knowledge need be demonstrated.

Grade-A answer to question 10.1

(a) Eurosceptics are mostly Conservative Party members who are worried about three big issues. Firstly, they do not want too much integration because this will mean loss of sovereignty and Britain will lose control over its affairs. Many of them also fear the loss of power to the French and Germans. Secondly, they are against the single currency because it means Britain will not control its own economic policy. Thirdly, they think the EU is undemocratic and believe it will transfer power to unaccountable institutions.

e This is an excellent grade-A answer that develops beyond the basic points. The candidate has managed to enlarge on three good points in a concise way.

(b) There are two ideas concerning sovereignty in the passage. The first is that Britain will lose sovereignty because it will have to accept decisions made in the Council of Ministers. However, this will not apply to decisions which need a unanimous vote. The other idea is that sovereignty will be pooled. This means that decisions in Europe are made jointly by all the members, so Britain will have a say in these decisions which affect all the members.

e Another accurate grade-A answer is given, where the concept of sovereignty is explained clearly in a response that goes a little beyond the extract.

(c) There are quite a number of responsibilities now controlled by the EU. The main one is trade and there has to be agreement on any tariffs or other restrictions on trade. There is also the Common Agricultural and Fisheries Policy which deals with taxes and subsidies in those industries. Each member is not allowed to give subsidies or levy taxes on its own. The Social Chapter means that there is European control over workers' rights. For example, there is a maximum working week of 47 hours and all countries must conform. The environment is deemed a European issue because environmental problems do not recognise national boundaries. There are things like cleanliness of beaches and sewage controls throughout Europe.

e A grade A is awarded again. The candidate also realises that time must be allowed for section (d). The list of examples is described with relevant illustrations.

(d) The idea of the single European currency is that all members of the EU should use the same currency and that this will avoid the expense of changing currencies for trade and tourism. Eleven countries have joined, but Britain has stayed out.

The main reason Eurosceptics oppose the single currency is that we will lose control over the running of the economy. We already do not control interest rates, but these will be transferred to a European Bank. It is possible that we will lose control over taxation policy too. European currency movements may also influence government spending.

But the main reason for opposition is that people believe it will eventually lead to a European super-state. This is because the loss of sovereignty over the economy will be followed by transfers of powers on other issues, such as taxation, health, education, defence and foreign policy. So they believe that the single currency is a kind of 'wooden horse of Troy' which will open up a whole series of other losses of British power.

Finally, there is the issue of the loss of the pound. Eurosceptics believe the pound is a symbol of British sovereignty and represents our history and culture. There is a great deal of nationalism about this. The queen's head on the currency would be lost and this represents the breaking of our traditions. Conservatives are very nationalist in their outlook, so this is a vital issue for them.

e This is a solid grade-A answer. There is no special economic analysis and this is not expected. The candidate has produced a good set of arguments, showing understanding and accuracy, and has addressed the question directly by referring at the end to Conservative philosophy.

e **The candidate was ready for the expected questions, responded to their exact wording and then extended the arguments. The answers are written in a concise, clear style, without any frills — ideal for saving time in the examination room. This is a high grade A overall.**

■ ■ ■

Question 10.2

(a) How is British sovereignty affected by membership of the EU? (20 marks)

(b) How has the issue of Britain's membership of the EU affected party politics? (20 marks)

Grade-A mark scheme for question 10.2 (65%+)

(a) Most of the various issues surrounding sovereignty should be explored fully. The loss of sovereignty should be analysed, especially with reference to the difference between qualified majority voting and unanimous voting in the Council of Ministers. There will be some differentiation between areas of policy where sovereignty is lost and where it has been retained. The concept that there is no ultimate loss of sovereignty because Britain has the option of leaving should be referred to. The effects on the sovereignty of parliament and the powers of the judiciary should be analysed, at least briefly. Analysis of the concept of pooled sovereignty may be mentioned but is not a requirement.

(b) There should be differentiation between the schisms which have opened both between and within parties. The divisions in the Conservative Party will be described. Labour's apparent unity (and hidden divisions) will be identified, as will the apparent unity among Liberal Democrats. Strong responses will refer to the fact that the Scottish and Welsh Nationalist parties both support closer membership of the EU. The single currency issue will be identified as crucial and briefly analysed. Reference to past disputes over Maastricht and Amsterdam or to current issues, such as the European Defence Force, are not necessary for a grade A but will be given additional credit if included.

■ ■ ■

Grade-B answer to question 10.2

(a) Sovereignty means ultimate political authority. It used to be that in Britain parliament was completely sovereign. This is not true any more because quite a lot of the sovereignty has been transferred to the EU. The sovereign body of the EU is the Council of Ministers, but Britain has only one seat on the Council and can be outvoted.

The issues that have been transferred to European sovereignty are: agriculture, trade arrangements, environmental protection, fishing and a good deal of employment and social law. It may be that there will be more transfers in rights over defence policy and taxation.

The most important case concerning sovereignty was the Factortame case. This meant that the Merchant Shipping Act — which had been passed by parliament — no longer stood because it was judged to be in conflict with European law. This showed that the British courts and parliament do not remain sovereign when in opposition with the EU. The European Court of Justice and the Council of Ministers has power to overrule what Britain does in the case shown above. Even if the government tried to maintain British power, it cannot do so if it is outvoted.

Finally, it has to be said that Britain can always leave the EU. If it did this, there is nothing the other members could do to stop it and this means that we have not lost sovereignty for all time.

e This high-level grade-B response mentions most of the key points, though it doesn't develop them enough. The candidate omits the issue of pooled sovereignty and has not described the difference between qualified majority and unanimous voting in the European Council or Council of Ministers. It is not always accurate to say Britain can be outvoted. The omission of two major points rules out a grade A. This is a predictable question and all aspects should have been learned.

(b) The most important aspect of party politics and the EU is that it has torn the Conservative Party apart. It has lost two elections in a row partly because the electorate sees the party as divided on the issue and this affects many votes. Many Tory members have left the party and some leading figures, such as Kenneth Clarke and Michael Heseltine, have fallen out of favour. This began under Margaret Thatcher but continued under John Major and William Hague. Hague patched things up, but he could not hide the division completely.

The most important issue for the Conservatives has been the single currency. They have opposed Britain joining it and were against the holding of a referendum on the issue. They are also concerned about losses of economic sovereignty and the European Defence Force. Both Labour and the Liberal Democrats are Euro-enthusiasts and have supported British membership of the single currency.

It is a strange fact that the British people are mostly sceptical about the EU, but they do not support the party — the Conservatives — which is most Eurosceptic. It is also true that the electorate is more interested in other issues such as the economy, health and education.

Now it is one of the biggest issues in British politics and is likely to be so for many years to come.

e Here is another good grade-B answer with a sound analysis of the situation in the Conservative Party. It is not a grade A because it is uncritical of the situation in the Labour Party and fails to identify the splits that exist there. There is no mention of smaller parties, especially the Nationalists. Analysis of the few issues mentioned is limited by lack of preparation and not enough broad knowledge. Top answers try to address all aspects of a question rather than concentrating on just one.

e **This is a grade-B candidate whose grasp of the subject and writing style is let down by two factors: points are undeveloped and key issues are omitted.**

■ ■ ■

Question 10.3

Study the following data and read the extract that follows:

Percentage of votes won in the 1999 UK elections to the European parliament

Party	Votes won (%)	Change from 1997 general election (%)
Conservative	35.8	+ 4.4
Labour	28.0	–16.0
Liberal Democrat	12.7	– 4.5
UK Independence Party	7.0	
Green	6.3	

In Great Britain the 1999 elections to the European Parliament produced one of the Labour Party's worst national election performances in living memory. Its 28% of the vote was marginally worse than Old Labour's nadir in the 1983 general election and a fall of 16.4% on the 1997 general election performance. The pattern of voting raises doubts about the durability of the electoral coalition of the traditional working-class Labour voters and the middle-class former Conservative voters to whom New Labour successfully appealed in 1997. The Conservatives emerged as the chief victors of the European elections, but the result marked only a limited revival in their fortunes. At 35.8%, the Conservative vote represented an increase of only 4.4% on their worst result in modern times in the last general election. The Conservatives were able to fight the election on an issue — membership of the euro — on which their position was more popular among the voters than that of the government.

Source: 'The 1999 European elections', Stephen Hopkins and Philip Lynch, *Politics Review*, Vol. 9, No. 2, November 1999.

(a) Why did the Conservatives do better in the elections shown than in the 1997 general election? (6 marks)

(b) Comment on the performance of the other parties in this election. (12 marks)

(c) What arguments have the Conservatives deployed in opposing British membership of the euro system? (22 marks)

Grade-A mark scheme for question 10.3 (65%+)

(a) Answers should concentrate on factors related to Europe. The revival was not reflected in opinion polls at the time. Responses should identify the euro issue as a main factor together with a general knowledge that the Conservative Eurosceptic position was more popular than the Labour and Liberal Democrat pro-European stances. The best answers will allude to the fact that there was a low turnout, which might have favoured the Conservatives. Reference might also be made to the extract's mention of the possible break-up of the Labour coalition, with some middle-class Conservative defectors returning to the party on the European issue specifically.

(b) The performance of all the other parties should be included in grade-A responses. There will be analyses of the decline of the Labour and Liberal Democrat votes since 1997. There will also be analysis of the strong performances by the UK Independence Party (UKIP) and the Greens. In each case, all plausible speculation will be credited if supported by reasonable evidence or valid political knowledge.

(c) The arguments against membership of the single currency will be explored and most of the following issues will be included: loss of economic sovereignty and flexibility; excessive influence from other member states and a central bank; loss of the pound as a symbol of British nationalism and independence; the danger that it will lead to federalism; and the possibility that the euro will prove to be a weak currency. Any other arguments which have been used by the Conservatives may be included. One or two omissions will be tolerated in a grade-A response, provided that those mentioned are well explained.

■ ■ ■

Grade-A answer to question 10.3

(a) The Conservative vote in the European parliamentary elections rose by 4.4% for a number of reasons. The first and most important was that they campaigned with policies which opposed British membership of the euro and further integration for Europe. Polls show that a majority of British people agree with these policies. The rise was small, but this may have been due to the fact that the UKIP may have split the anti-Europe vote. There was also a low turnout. Many believe Labour voters are less likely to vote than Conservatives, so this partly explained the Conservative victory.

e This is a solid grade-A response with an excellent comment on how the UKIP vote split the Conservative vote. The candidate identifies the effect of the low turnout in an answer that addresses the question directly and fully.

(b) I will look at each of the parties in turn and attempt to explain why they performed as they did in these elections.

Firstly, it was a bad result for Labour. Its vote went down from 44% in the general election to 28% in this one. This was partly because of a successful Eurosceptic campaign by the Tories and also because of the low turnout. Many Labour voters probably stayed at home out of complacency. The Labour leaders said voters were apathetic because they were so happy with the economic performance of the government and did not bother to vote. Labour was doing well in the opinion polls in 1999 so it could not have been just unpopularity.

The Liberal Democrats also did badly with a small fall in support. Again, it might have been due to the low turnout, but it may also have been because Liberals are pro-Europe and this was not popular at the time.

The UKIP mounted a big anti-Europe campaign and was well financed by some wealthy businessmen. It probably stole some votes from the Conservatives.

The Greens improved on their tiny vote in general elections, mainly due to the more proportional electoral system, which encouraged people to vote for a small party. They also have strong European policies as the environment is a major European issue.

e This comprehensive answer addresses the full range of the question. A good deal of additional knowledge is applied and some excellent points are made about, for example, the Greens and the electoral system and the funding of UKIP. The candidate had obviously noted that these sorts of relevant extra points can win good marks. The structure of the answer is simple, clear and direct, and the student earns a high grade A.

(c) The Conservative Party is generally Eurosceptic, and it is issues of the euro and Britain's membership of EMU which are most important. Many Conservatives have a number of objections to 'Britain and the euro'. They believe that it will lead to a great loss of sovereignty, independence and national identity. The pound is an important part of British culture and tradition, so they do not want to lose it. They argue that we would lose a great deal of power to German bankers.

Eurosceptics also believe that the British economy is not suitable to be closely integrated with Europe and suggest that joining the euro will cause inflation and unemployment. They say our economy is more closely linked with the US. There is the question too of taxation. At the moment, we control our own taxes, but Tories believe that if we have the euro we will have to bring in European taxes (a stupid argument as some European taxes are lower).

Finally, they argue that the euro is a weak currency whereas the pound is strong. If we go into the euro, import prices will have to rise because the currency would be worth less. Of course, this is only short term, and in future the pound might be weak and the euro strong.

But the really important argument is independence. Conservatism stands for a strong, independent nation, free from outside influence and able to shape its own destiny. Conservatives fear that the euro will lead to a federal Europe and even a full-scale European super-state. So for them it is a much wider issue.

e First, let me express a word of caution. The candidate criticises the Conservative view, albeit in a light-hearted way. This should not be done. The question does not ask for a criticism of the Conservative view, but asks for that view to be described and explained. Students should avoid expressing their own political views and instead take a detached, balanced view and stick to the requirements of the question. While an assessment of arguments is sometimes asked for, questions in AS Politics never ask for personal views on political issues. That aside, this is a solid, grade-A answer. Most of the key points are mentioned and each is explained well.

e **The candidate responds effectively to the data, has a clear style of writing, structures the answers well and divides up the points by using plenty of paragraph breaks. There is evidence of thorough preparation for the general questions on the euro which merits a good grade A.**